THE FUTURE OF THE WORLD

STUDIES IN BIBLICAL THEOLOGY

A series of monographs designed to provide clergy and laymen with the best work in biblical scholarship both in this country and abroad

Second Series · 23

THE FUTURE
OF THE WORLD

An Exegetical Study of Revelation 19.11-22.15

MATHIAS RISSI

ALEC R. ALLENSON INC.
635 EAST OGDEN AVENUE
NAPERVILLE, ILL.

TO JOHN BRIGHT

72 - 186007

0 9 8 1

The English text of this book is an expanded and revised version of the original German edition, *Die Zukunft der Welt. Eine exegetische Studie über Johannesoffenbarung 19.11– 22.15*, Verlag Friedrich Reinhardt, Basel, 1966.

ISBN 0 – 8401 – 3073 – 2

Published by Alec R. Allenson Inc.
Naperville, Ill.
Printed in Great Britain

CONTENTS

ABBREVIATIONS

CBQ	*Catholic Biblical Quarterly*
Comm.	*Commentary* (on Revelation)
EvTh	*Evangelische Theologie*
Interpr.	*Interpretation*
JBL	*Journal of Biblical Literature*
JTS	*Journal of Theological Studies*
KEK	*Kritisch—Exegetischer Kommentar über das Neue Testament* (Meyer-Kommentar)
NT	*Novum Testamentum*
NTS	*New Testament Studies*
RB	*Revue Biblique*
Stud.Neotest.	*Studia Neotestamentica*
TDNT	*Theological Dictionary of the New Testament*, ET of G.Kittel and G.Friedrich (eds.),
TWNT	*Theologisches Wörterbuch zum Neuen Testament*
ThLZ	*Theologische Literaturzeitung*
ThZ	*Theologische Zeitschrift*
VT	*Vetus Testamentum*
ZAW	*Zeitschrift für die alttestamentliche Wissenschaft*
ZNW	*Zeitschrift für die neutestamentliche Wissenschaft*

PREFACE

Although the eschatological hopes of the apostle Paul have been analysed in innumerable studies, biblical scholarship has more or less tended to neglect the eschatological concepts of the Book of Revelation. This is probably an outgrowth of the deep mistrust that has surrounded this apocalypse of the New Testament almost since the beginning of the history of its interpretation. It may be because scholars have been troubled by what appears to be its 'superficially Christianized Judaism', especially in its statements with regard to what lies beyond history;[1] or it may be that they have not known what to make of the idea of an 'intermediate Messianic kingdom', which appears in the entire New Testament only in this book;[2] or perhaps it is that, in their concern with the origin of the various materials that have been built into the work, they have forgotten the work as a whole and have failed to catch what it is trying to say;[3] or it may be because they have sought to harmonize the special form that the eschatology of John takes with general Christian conceptions and, in so doing, have deprived it of its peculiar quality;[4] or, finally, it may be that, blinded by their own philosophical conceptions with regard to the world and history, they simply have no eye for the immensity of these seemingly fantastic pictures, because their philosophy leaves no room for any real hope for the future of the world.[5]

Nevertheless, anyone who takes the trouble to listen will discover with what astounding, truly prophetic power John has shaped the images of the future in the light of the historical revelation of Christ.[6]

The present study is an attempt to take John seriously, to

meditate upon what he says, and to follow him even where he makes it difficult for us to do so, and where we are sorely tempted to give it up and travel on more accustomed paths. Only so will we come to recognize what fascinated him and overpowered him, and what it was that he particularly wanted to say.

The structure of this study is determined by the structure of the texts themselves. It is obvious that at Rev. 19.11ff. a new section of the book begins which leads from an explanation of the history of the church and the world into a portrayal and an interpretation of Christ's second coming and of the 'history' of the final perfection following his parousia.

In these last visions of the book two stages of eschatological hope can be discerned: the events between the parousia and the end of this present world, together with the last judgment (19.11–20.15); and then the creation of the new world, which follows (21.1–22.5).

In the introductory chapter I rely upon parts of my article, 'The Kerygma of the Revelation to John' (*Interpr.* 22, 1968, pp.3-17).

I wish to acknowledge my deepest gratitude to Professor John Bright, not only for his help in making the translation of this book readable, but also for his true friendship and the continuous intellectual stimulation I have experienced in 'the house of the cannonball'! Special thanks go also to Mrs F.S. Clark who typed the manuscript and accompanied my undertaking with unceasing patience, interest, and humour.

INTRODUCTION

Before we study the eschatological views of the Revelation to John, it might be helpful to consider first some aspects of its message as a whole. Since no other book of the New Testament has found so many entirely different interpretations as the Revelation, it is not easy to present its message in a few pages.[1] The difficulties arise especially out of the particular form of the work: its message is disclosed in visionary imagery[2] which is to be deciphered trait by trait on the basis of the underlying traditions of the Old Testament and Jewish apocalypticism.[3] Though a consensus of interpretation has not yet been reached concerning either the overall conception or the details, the time of a bizarre world-history and church-history interpretation which discovered the fulfilment of the Johannine visions in specific historical events ought to have passed.[4] John has certainly written for his contemporaries; but the question remains open as to how far the author refers to historical situations and events of his time or to a future development of an end-history prophetically predicted, or whether he wants to disclose the meaning of all history through the provision of an entirely mythical history of the end.[5]

1

Although this is not the place to deal with the historical problems attaching to the Revelation, it is necessary at this point to say a few words regarding them. I take the whole book to be basically a literary unity, written by one author.[6] Cogent linguistic, stylistic, and theological reasons against this view cannot be found.[7] The book was not published — like the

Jewish apocalypses — under the name of an important godly man of the past who 'prophesied' past and future history, for the author writes under his own name: John. This name, however, does not help us in our attempt to identify him, for we do not know who this John really was. Witnesses of the early church frequently mention John the son of Zebedee as the author of the Revelation, but their testimony is open to question[8] — although it would not be fair to exclude this possibility altogether.[9]

More precision is possible regarding the time of composition, for traces of the earliest history of our book seem to be visible in ch.17. In 17.1-18 we can clearly distinguish between the work of two different hands: the original Johannine draft of the vision (17.1-6)with its original interpretation (17.7-9a,18), and a secondary reinterpretation of the visionary beast (17.9b-17). This understanding of 17.1-18 is the result of the observation of several inconsistencies which make its unity questionable:

1. In comparison with the interpretation of the woman in verse 18 and also in view of the brevity of all other vision interpretations in Revelation, the explanation of the beast exhibits an extraordinary *length*. 2. Only in 17.9b-17 do we find a *double* interpretation of a vision (the heads are hills and emperors). 3. The interpretation of the series of emperors *destroys the unity* of the visionary picture, since the sixth emperor (i.e., the sixth head of the beast) is present at the time of the alleged composition of Revelation, although according to 17.10 the beast itself is not yet present. 4. The seven heads of the original vision did not suffice for the purposes of the secondary interpreter. He therefore introduced an *eighth* emperor. 5. He also interprets 'the waters' as an element of John's vision (17.15: 'the waters you have seen'), although the waters *do not appear* in the vision itself (17.3-6), but only in the words introducing it, which are taken from Old Testament descriptions of Babylon. 6. According to the later interpreter, the woman sits on the *heads* of the beast (17.9b), but not in the original version. 7. The idea of an *eschatological battle* between the Lamb and his enemies is contrary to the christology of Revelation and appears only here in 17.14.

This whole artificial reinterpretation is based upon Jewish

apocalyptic technique (otherwise not employed in the Book of Revelation): history is 'predicted' from a fictitious standpoint in the past. The unknown secondary interpreter pretends to be writing at the time of the sixth emperor of the City on the Seven Hills, i.e., Rome (17.10), but he is already well informed about the destiny of the seventh and eighth emperors! It is therefore no far-fetched assumption that he wants to put his own interpretation of past history, in the form of a prediction, into the mouth of a prophet who lived at the time of the sixth emperor. Since the original author of the Revelation wrote his book under his own name, it is more than probable that the secondary interpreter referred to *him* in 17.10.[10]

According to the secondary interpreter the eighth emperor will represent the beast, i.e., the Antichrist, who has already appeared among the seven emperors. Since he exempts the sixth and seventh emperors from being the beast (17.10f.), the beast must have been one of the first five emperors. This is obviously a reference to the well-known persecutor of the Christians: Nero. Stories were told after Nero's death which declared that he did not die and that, later on, he would come back from the underworld in order to march against Rome together with his satraps. This saga is undoubtedly used in 17.16f. The eighth emperor is none other than Nero *redivivus*. The secondary interpreter combined both the traditional account of the battle of Christ's enemies with the Lamb and their march against Rome. He did it in an unfortunate way, for he speaks first of the complete defeat of the Lamb's enemies and then nevertheless of their march against Rome (17.12-17).

Nero *redivivus* can only be Domitian, the second persecutor of the church in the first century. This 'prophetic' interpretation is in perfect agreement with history. Thus the seventh emperor is Titus, who indeed reigned only 'a short time', namely, two years (17.10). He and his father, Vespasian (the sixth emperor), did not hurt the church. They are therefore not identified with the beast. Since the emperors of the *interregnum* (Galba, Otho, Vitellius) are not to be counted (cf. Suetonius) in this list of the official representatives of the Roman Empire, the fifth emperor must be Nero, the fourth Claudius, the third Caligula, the second Tiberius, the first Augustus. The message the unknown interpreter of ch.17 wanted to convey to his brothers is well understandable. He wanted to alert and to comfort the church in its persecution: Domitian is the Antichrist; but do not despair, for this means that the end is at hand, Christ is coming soon! He felt compelled by the circumstances to undertake a new edition of John's book, whose relevance he tried to sharpen by his interpolations.

The other trace of the secondary interpreter's expectations can be found in the famous number riddle in Rev. 13.17b,18. It is quite obvious here that something has been inserted, for the description of the Antichrist (Rev. 13.10) is concluded by a word of admonition, as is the description of the pseudo-prophet (13.18a). But then an additional interpretation follows, which is introduced by a new word of warning. This interpretation is added to the vision of the beast from the earth, but it refers to the beast from the sea. Not only this, but also the meaning of the number suggests an interpolation. The number 666 is called the number of a man and stands for a name, as Rev. 13.17b shows. The old assumption that the number refers to Caesar Nero is certainly correct; it refers to Nero *redivivus*, as we have already seen. The sum of the numerical value of the Hebrew letters of Caesar Nero is 666. The defective way of writing which has to be presupposed has been confirmed recently in a document of the second year of Nero's reign. The unknown secondary interpreter has certainly altered the original meaning of the figure of Antichrist in ch.13, for John did not speak here of a man but of a superhuman satanic reality. The number also links ch.13 with ch.17, for the number 666 is at the same time a 'triangle number'; i.e., 666 is the sum of all numbers from 1 to 36, and 36 is the sum of all numbers from 1 to 8. According to well-known triangle number speculation, in the Hellenistic world, the number 8 has the same meaning as 666. Thus 666 points to an 'eighth one' with whom the Antichrist of ch.13 must be identical, that is to say, to the eighth emperor of the Roman Empire in 17.11. The secondary interpreter therefore urges his church to consider the meaning of the apocalyptic number. The same man has also inserted the remark 'the number of his name' in Rev. 13.17b and 15.2 (but he forgot to do the same in Rev. 14.11 and 16.2).

The work of the secondary interpreter is probably reflected in the statements of early church fathers (Irenaeus, *Adv. haer.*

5, 30, 3; Eusebius, *Hist. eccl.* 3, 18, 1; Hieronymus, *De vir. ill.* 3, 8) who took the time of the second edition of Revelation to be the time of its original composition. The unknown interpreter, however, still knew exactly when John had written his book and therefore dates it back to the time of the sixth emperor, Vespasian. Since the editor indicates that the seventh emperor 'has not yet come', it is likely that he points to the fact that the seventh emperor (Titus) will take over soon. The probable date of John's work is thus the last years of Vespasian's reign, i.e., c.75-79.

Over against this, A. Strobel has recently attempted to show that Domitian is to be understood as the sixth emperor, 'who is now'.[11] He begins to count the series of emperors with Christ's death; he is, however, unable to include Tiberius, who outlived Jesus, but begins his count with Caligula in order to arrive at Domitian as the sixth emperor 'in the series'. Against his thesis there is also the fact that the death of Jesus is not the only starting point in John's conception of the end of history (p.437). John can point to the death of Jesus as the decisive victory, but also to his birth and his ascension, thus to the entire historical Christ event 'viewed as' a unity (12.5).[12] The atmosphere created by Caligula's plan to erect a statue of the emperor in the temple in Jerusalem is no argument for Strobel's thesis, for not only is there no trace of this plan to be found in Revelation, but in John's conception of the matter it had nothing of the Antichrist about it since, in his view, the earthly Jerusalem with its temple is written off as 'Sodom and Egypt', or 'the world'. Moreover, it cannot be proved that ἔπεσαν (17.10) can refer only to violent death (p.441), while the fact that two out of the five emperors in Strobel's series were not assassinated at all (how widely the rumours of their assassination were believed we do not know) is a further factor making for uncertainty (pp.439f.). Nor can it be proved that the prophetic idea of the 'last week' (of seventy years) was a guiding principle for the author of Revelation, just because of the significance that the number 7 had for him, and because of his taking over the 'Danielic expression' δεῖ. What is astonishing is precisely the complete absence in Revelation (even with reference to the millennium!) of any allusion to such widespread week-speculations — in spite of the enormous signifi-

cance that the number 7 has (which, however, has a different
basis). It is therefore hard to understand why, in this conception of the matter, an eighth emperor had to be introduced, and
why the final embodiment of the Antichrist — which, according to Strobel, was imminently expected — was not seen in the
seventh, i.e., the ruler following Domitian (between 96 and
100). That would even have corresponded to the vision of the
seven heads.

It is much easier to assume that a redactor has inserted his
interpretation into the apocalypse, which was written during
Vespasian's reign, and placed it in the mouth of the original
author as a prophecy (just as the pseudonymous Jewish
apocalypses placed words in the mouth of some godly man of
the distant past). The computation is thus seen to be a *vatici-
nium ex eventu* with an exact 'prediction' of the succession of
emperors: the first five are Augustus, Tiberius, Caligula,
Claudius, and Nero; the sixth, 'who is now here', is Vespasian;
the seventh, who 'will remain only a little while', is Titus (only
from 79 to 81!); and the eighth, in whom the Beast out of the
underworld finds his embodiment, is Domitian.[13]

2

The task accepted by John in his vocation to be a prophet
(1.9ff.) consists essentially in the *interpretation of history*,
more precisely the interpretation of present and future history:
'Write down what you have seen, namely, what is and what will
take place after that' (1.19).[14] But his way of interpretation is
not the way of the Jewish apocalyptists who undertake to show
the predetermined, divine plan of history for Israel from a
fictitious viewpoint in the past. He thus writes in his own name,
not under a pseudonym, and he does not start somewhere in
the past as a fictitious 'prophet', but with the eschatological
action of God in Jesus Christ which stamps for him the present
and the future. The period of history interpreted by John is
limited by the redemptive event of the death and resurrection
of the Lamb and his parousia (cf. 5 and 19.11ff.). Moreover, it
is important to notice that John does not predict specific
historical events, as is the case in Jewish apocalypticism. He
rather interprets the true meaning and nature of the history
with which he is concerned in terms of a traditional imagery

long since known and taken over particularly from the Old Testament and also from Jewish concepts.[15]

The exposition of the nature of this final historical period is strictly theological. The great vision of the world ruler and the Lamb, therefore, precedes all the other visions (4-5).

God is infinitely remote and sublime, seen, above all, in his function as 'he who is sitting on the throne', the king. The *pantokrator* is in command of the whole world as its creator (4.6) who, surrounded by his heavenly hosts in his terrifying and immovable majesty, governs the earth's chaotic history.

But God does not remain in this remoteness; in the seer's view he is the God whom we already know, because he has revealed himself. He is the one who had already made himself known in the past, who is revealing himself, and who will do so tomorrow. He is not only 'he who is and was', but also — as he is called in a characteristic transformation of Exodus 3.14 — 'he who is to come' (1.4), 'the beginning and the end', 'the Alpha and Omega' (1.8). God is no static *fatum,* no fixed principle of history, but 'the living God' (7.2).[16] In the course of history he reveals his grace and his wrath (1.4; 16.1): grace and judgment characterize his image in ch.4, for his throne is framed by a rainbow, the ancient symbol of mercy, and by 'lightnings, voices, and thunder', signs of wrath which proceed from his throne (4.3,5)! He has set a goal for history, and with 'right-eousness' he leads the 'ways' of the nations toward the goal: that they may come and worship him (15.4).

The most important and central confession, however, states that God is the 'father' of Jesus Christ (1.6; 2.28; 3.5,21; 14.1). God's fatherhood is referred only to Christ, who lives in an exclusive relationship with God. For the Father speaks his word through Christ (19.13), and also acts through him, execu-ting his will (6.1ff.). This is particularly evident in the second part of the great vision in chs.4 and 5: God rules the world as the king of the nations and holds in his right hand a book sealed with seven seals (cf. Ezek. 2.9f.), which no one can open — no one 'in heaven, on earth and under the earth', that is, in all the realms of creation. 'And I wept much' (5.4), for the world and its history — left to itself — is disastrous. But then — expressed in the framework of an ancient oriental pattern of 'authori-zation'[17] — John is told that the execution of God's plan is

bestowed upon the messianic king promised in the Old Testament, 'the lion of the tribe of Judah, the root of David' (Gen.
49.9; Isa. 11.1,10; cf. Jer. 23.5; 33.15).[18] It is of the highest
importance to notice that this ruler is described as the redeemer, as a lamb who had been slain and who is wearing seven
horns and seven eyes, symbols of divine omnipotence and
omniscience. This commission of the Lamb to execute the will
of God discloses the character of God's will and of the sealed
book as his redemptive plan for history, because in and through
the Lamb, God is at work for the salvation of man.

3

To *Christ* through whom the Father is speaking and operating,
divine predicates are attributed. He can be called 'the First and
the Last', 'Alpha and Omega', the 'Beginning of creation' (1.17;
3.14; 22.13), who is sitting with his Father on the Father's
throne (3.21; cf. 11.15; 12.10). And his visionary shape is
described according to God's appearance in Daniel 7.9: his
head, his hairs are 'white like wool, as white as snow' (1.14). He
is worshipped as his Father (5.13; 7.10; 12.10). And yet his
dominion of the world does not rest on his divine status, but on
his work accomplished in history; through his life on earth he
has overcome the rebellion of the whole world. This victory is
the presupposition of his dominion: 'He has won the victory
and is [therefore] able to open the book' (5.5).[19] The word
ἐνίκησεν marks the centre of the Revelation's christology.
What it means is crystal clear from the context. First of all, the
aorist form points to the fact that the victory has already taken
place once and for all at a historical moment in the past. That
νικᾶν is used without an object proves his victory to be unlimited and absolute. It is no accident that the same characteristics are applied to Christ's victory in the other passage,
3.21: ἐνίκησα. What this victory means is expounded in the
interpreting hymn 5.9:[20] 'Thou art worthy to take the book
and to open the seals, for [ὅτι] thou wast slain and hast
purchased men for God by thy blood ....' The *victory*
took place when he *died* and his *death* was the act of man's
redemption. The victor thus appears in the astonishing and
paradoxical shape of a lamb with the marks of slaughter
upon him. The ruler who shows the signs of his omnipotence

(seven horns) and who is the bearer of the divine spirit (seven eyes) was slain as a lamb! The Old Testament imagery of 'the Lamb' designates him as a sacrificial animal that dies for the atonement (5.9; 1.5). His sacrifice is not a mythical sacrifice, but the death of Jesus Christ on the cross (11.8). His death occurred for the sake of man and caused the deliverance of man from all bondage to the world and its mighty powers (5.9; 14.4), so that they are enabled to conquer the enemy themselves (12.10). The deliverance is fulfilled as the forgiveness of all sins, wherein his love is revealed (1.5; cf. 7.14; 21.14). Here in 5.5 (cf. 3.21) we feel the heartbeat of the whole christology of John. The understanding of this concept of Christ's victory is of the greatest consequence for the interpretation of the entire book.[21] It is in his death that Christ overcomes his enemies, the world — not on a bloody eschatological battlefield, not through condemnation and annihilation, but through redemption. The word νικᾶν, therefore, never designates any destructive judgment upon the enemies. John has consistently maintained this view throughout the whole book. For him there is only *one* victory of Christ; it was won in the past and resulted in the debilitation of all enemy powers, once and for all. Thus John knows no necessity for a perennial repetition of Christ's victory nor for an eschatological completion of his decisive past victory. This view is confirmed by the visions of the very end of history in which the entire hostile world prepares a final battle against Christ and where we would again expect to find the term νικᾶν employed with reference to the victorious Christ (16.12-21 and 19.11-21). But because the victory is already brought about, there will be no eschatological battle: the agglomerations of all enemy powers break down without any combat-action of Christ.[22]

From this concept we meet the term νικᾶν also applied to the church and the Antichrist. On the ground of Christ's victory the church may 'be victorious' too. Her victory consists in the fact that she does not succumb any more to the temptations of the world[23] and that she does not worship the enemy.[24]

In the sharpest contrast to this there stands the νικᾶν of the Antichrist in 11.7; 13.7 and especially in 6.2. The decisive difference is not taken into account if we interpret the rider on the white horse (6.1f.) either as a redemptive action of God or Christ, or as a 'personification of the divine judgment' that takes place already proleptically in history, that is, as a representation of 'the eschatological judgment under its theological aspect of the divine victory', an interpretation which should connect 6.1f. with 19.11-16. [25] This interpretation neglects completely the main difference between these two visions: νικᾶν is not applied to the image of the judgment in 19.11-16f. because the victory of Christ has long since been won on the cross! The characteristics of the Antichrist's victory in 6.2, however, indicate that his victory can never be accomplished; in spite of all his victories (νικῶν) the Antichrist has to be continually after new victories (καὶ ἵνα νικήσῃ)! For his victories will never cancel the victory of the cross![26] The closest parallel to that is given in 11.7 and 13.7: the victory over the church is granted to the Antichrist by God (ἐδόθη : *passivum divinum*), but the victims of these victories are elevated to heaven as the real victors (12.11; 15.2).[27]

The vision of ch.12 mentions the same paradox of Christ's victory. The defenceless Christ-child is seen in the realm of the dragon's power, out of which he has to be 'caught up unto God and to his throne' (12.5). In an astonishing abridgement of history, the whole lifetime of Jesus is passed over in order to demonstrate the utter inconceivability of God's victory in the Child whose way leads into the sphere of the Dragon and even into the ultimate peril of death mentioned in the interpreting hymn 12.10f. Here and now 'is come victory and strength and the kingdom of our God and the power of his Christ'. Appointed by God, Christ is victorious as the powerless, sacrificial lamb who loves us and has become the destiny of the world!

Thus, in the midst of history, the meaning, purpose, and goal of history has come to light in the eschatological event which has brought about the fulfilment of the Old Testament promises. For God has overcome his enemies through their redemption in Christ. This is the presupposition for the understanding of the entire process of redemptive history.

4

Although John does not reflect upon the role of *the Holy Spirit*, it is obvious that he believes that the presence of Christ is experienced in the presence of the Spirit. So when Christ is speaking to the churches the Spirit is speaking (cf. 2.1,7; 19.10). The presence of the Spirit is symbolized in the image of the seven flaming torches immediately before the divine throne (4.5). With that, the Spirit is characterized as God's Spirit (cf. Gen. 15.17 and Ezek. 1.13). Therefore the Spirit is mentioned together with God and Christ as the divine giver of the eschatological gifts, grace and peace (1.4). Particularly related to the church — seen as a circle of seven churches — the Spirit is connected with the number seven, which points to the fullness of the Spirit, and at the same time to his appearance in every individual church.[28]

5

God is confronted with his creation in its threefold structure as the *world*, the *church*, and *Israel*.

John is not interested in any cosmological speculation, for the 'cosmos' in his view is *the world of man* (11.15). Very often he uses the term 'earth' in order to designate the arena of history. This place is the place of a universal rebellion. 'All those who dwell upon the earth' live in a constant contradiction to God — secretly or publicly — and attempt to live by themselves.[29] Their political leaders are called 'the kings of the earth' according to Ps. 2.2; 89.28, who wage war against God (16.14; 17.18), trying to overpower Christ and his church up to the last day (13.16f.; 19.19ff.). The rebellious world attempts to enforce world-wide unity and uniformity to the last fanatical consequence (13.16f.).

The visible surface of the godless world and its history, however, is covered by a thin skin, and when it bursts open, terrifying realities creep out of its uncanny depths. Its mysterious strength, temptation, and seduction appear in the powers who present themselves to the inner eyes of the seer as perverted counter-images and antagonists of God, Christ, and the Spirit as an odd trinity of *Dragon*, *Antichrist*, and *Antispirit* with all their host of evil spirits (chs.12-13).

Whoever separates himself from God delivers himself up to these powers. Man needs this strange transcendence when he loses God, for he is religious by nature. Religious imagination forms a unifying band around the world, for religion in general is the attempt of man to produce an 'image' of God which in truth is an image of these transcendent powers, of the beast (13.14f.). This 'image' is by no means a subjective idea only, but, rather, speaks objectively and causes death for those who will not worship it (13.15). The only danger to the religious world is the totally unreligious church of the Lamb, which does not live by the power of the world and its principalities, but only by the gifts of the Lamb.

While chs.12 and 13 describe the mysterious background of history, chs.17 and 18 point to the concrete activities of these powers within temporal history. John experiences the obsession of the world in the *Roman Empire* and its emperors who represent the beast and the whore (Babylon). His interpretation of the beast in ch.17, however, shows that John does not identify every Roman emperor as an incorporation of the Antichrist. When he says, 'The beast was already here', he certainly thinks of Nero and his persecution of the church. But even when he expects to see another, ultimate, Antichrist-representative on the Roman throne,[30] he does not demonize the whole Roman Empire: right now, he says, the beast is not visible (17.8). And even when he describes the destruction of Rome, we feel his deep regret for the beauty, wealth, and radiating world of art misled by godless powers.

Nevertheless, this world in its constant attempt to renounce the Creator is kept under the rule of God, and his plan of salvation cannot be disturbed. The government of God in his Son is described in three series of visions: seals, trumpets, and bowls. The seal and trumpet visions reveal the essence of history interpreted from different aspects, whereas the bowl visions, which are closely related to the latter (based upon the same traditional pattern), show a more advanced state of the judgments of God which affect the whole world without limitations. The bowl visions depict the nature of the last period of history as characterized by the scheme of deterioration, which appears also in Jewish and Christian expectations. In these visions God in his sanctity opposes the world which lives by itself and breaks its unity by revealing the whole questionable nature of its glory and might through his judgments. And yet it is essential that the sealed book should be opened by nobody but the Lamb (6.1ff.), that is, the execution of the divine plan takes place under the sign of Christ's cross, under the gospel and not the law. In other words, the judgments are to be understood as an expression of the 'wrath of the *Lamb*', that is to say, of the divine love (cf. 3.19). Their goal is never destruction and annihilation, but *repentance*, return to God. Four times John speaks of repentance in the judgment visions: 9.20f.; 16.9,11. To be sure, the formulation is negative: 'and they did not repent. . . .' But I do not think that John wanted to show by that the impossibility of repentance and the hopeless abandonment of the world by God, but, rather, to point to the *responsibility* of the world, that is, rejection of repentance entangles man inevitably in still deeper judgment. By using the apocalyptic phrase δεῖ γενέσθαι (1.1;4.7;22.6;[11.5;13.10]), he does not base this compulsion on any 'law of history', but solely on the will of God. Even the church is not exempt from the demand for repentance as long as she takes part in the world. The church, too, is constantly jeopardized by the possibility of rejection of repentance (cf. 3.21ff.).

This openness of history to decision rests upon the *word* directed to man by God. The offer of repentance precedes the judgment explicitly in the small· but important paragraph 14.6ff. God sends his angel 'in the midst of heaven' (where everybody can see him, according to ancient ideas), 'having an everlasting gospel to preach' unto the unbelievers[31] who are circumscribed by the cosmic number 4. It is the common expectation of the New Testament church that the message of salvation must be preached to all nations before the end.[32] On the ground of this proclamation the angel calls the world into the freedom of repentance and the worship of the Creator (14.7; cf. 13.4,8). God gives the freedom for decision. The nations thus gain an independent significance, for they are not merely the framework of the history of God's people as in Jewish apocalypticism. God has not only a purpose for his people, but also a genuine promise of salvation for the nations, since the redemptive will of 'the kings of the nations' will guide the nations to his worship (15.3f.). With that, John takes over universalistic, prophetic hopes of the Old Testament: 'All nations shall come and worship before thee' (15.4; cf. Ps. 86.9; Jer. 16.19). His hopes are based upon the victory of the Lamb which enables him to see through all the veils of history to the very goal of the Lamb's victory: '. . . and *every creature* . . . heard I praise God and the Lamb' (15.13).

6

The place where the good news is accepted and where a voice is provided for it is *the church of Jesus Christ*. She sings already the new eschatological hymn of the Lamb's victory (14.3) which has freed her from the world and its powers. She holds fast to the word of God, to the testimony of Jesus Christ, to his name, and to faith in him.[33] The ground of her salvation and the sign of her election is no longer the law (as in Judaism), but the gospel, and the Lord himself.

Whoever keeps the word of Jesus, the chief 'witness' of God, becomes a witness himself. Therefore, the church can present herself in exemplary fashion in the form of 'the two witnesses' (11.3ff.).[34] As witness to the Lamb the church is a promise for all nations, for the church herself is called out of all nations (5.9; 14.4). Thus she is a community of 'priests' (1.6; 5.10) and an ἀπαρχή ('first fruits'), bearing the promise for all men (14.4). Through her the world is confronted with God. The church has therefore become the destiny of world history, for the position that is taken with regard to her and her testimony determines the future of man.[35]

In the midst of the church, in her history on earth, the eschatological redemption of man is at work. For the Lord is in her midst as the powerful eschatological Son of Man and High Priest (1.13),[36] and as the Lamb (14.1). Where the church exists, there the eschatological world is already present within the old world: the church stands on the holy eschatological ground of Mount Zion (14.1ff.; cf. Isa. 10.12).

Jesus communicates with his church through his Spirit (1.7; 19.10). In his love he grants her forgiveness and freedom from all accusations (1.5; 12.10), and true eternal life (3.1f.; 21.6; 22.17). She experiences already the power of Christ's victory (5.9; 14.4) as a community of kings (1.6,9; 5.10; cf. Exod. 19.6). But her reign is entirely bound to the Lord and consists in her powerful prayer (8.2-6) and proclamation of the word, the rejection of which issues in judgment (11.5f.). John stands in the tradition of the early church, which believes: '. . . whoever hears you hears me and whoever rejects you rejects myself and him who has sent me' (Luke 10.16).

Since the particular history of the church, especially as described in chs.12-14 and the three interludes (7; 10.1-11.13; 16.15), is imbedded in world history, even the church has to take part in the judgments, being exempt only from events that lead into complete despair (9.4-6). But she is able to endure because she is sealed with the sign of protection under the name of the Lamb and his Father (7.1-8; 14.1).[37]

The church lives, however, in particular vexations and in jeopardy of her relationship to Christ through the temptations offered by the religious world which tries to undermine the life and teaching of the church from within (2-3). The other danger which threatens her from without is that of oppression and bloody persecution (6.9-11). The church of Pergamum has already suffered a persecution — probably through some religious fanatics who killed Antipas (2.13) in the famous cult place of Zeus and Asclepius, which is called 'the throne of Satan'. Some passages also point to a persecution organized by the Roman state (6.16 [Nero]) whose revival John fears in 17.1-9a,18 as a principal expression of the enmity of the state against the church. In agreement with Old Testament and Jewish expectations he sees a division taking place in history, not because the church separates itself from the world, but because the world increasingly resists the witnesses of Christ (11.7-10; 13.16f.; 17.6; 18.24). As a symbol for the ultimate climax of this division, the Revelation employs the image of an eschatological war (11.7; 13.7), and especially of the battle on the mythical 'mount of the assembly', Harmagedon (16.16),[38] and of Gog's final battle (19.17-21; cf. Ezek. 39). In contrast to Jewish expectations, John by no means sees the church taking part in the eschatological war, for the victory is long since won and the battle does not take place, only a divine judgment (16.17-21; 19.17-21). Nevertheless, the church can fall under the strokes of the enemies, for she is still the people of the sacrificial Lamb, 'who follows the Lamb wherever he goes' (14.4)! But not even death can separate her from salvation. For the believers to die means to be delivered from the great tribulation and to have a place in the presence of God and the Lamb (in the heavenly temple, 7.9-17; under the heavenly altar, 6.9; at the shores of the crystal sea in heaven, 15.2). They — not the beast that causes their death — are the real victors![39]

7

The Revelation puts those *Jews* who do not believe in the Lamb and despise the church in a strange twilight beside and between the world and the church. 'Jew' remains a name of honour of the elect, but the real Jew ought to accept the new revelation in Jesus Christ. If he separates himself from the church, he loses his relationship with God and becomes a member of the synagogue which confuses God with Satan (2.9; 3.9). His history has become the history of divine rejection. Chapter 11 deals especially with the fate of Israel-Jerusalem, the town of the temple people. John sees Israel divided by the challenge of faith. The unbelievers are rejected, and only a remnant still belongs to God's people (11.1f.). Through the crucifixion of Christ and through continuous unrepentance, Jerusalem is secularized like Sodom and Egypt. Thus it serves as a mirror of man's situation in general.[40] Here, as in the whole world, the two witnesses of Christ, the believers of Israel and the nations — as the church of the Lamb — proclaim the word of God. John does not expect the solution of the Jewish problem within the limits of world history, but, rather, from a new creative intervention of God beyond history. The believing part of Israel, however, plays an important role in the church as her foundation (7.1-8) and is worthy of a special protection until the parousia of Christ (12.6ff.).

8

The faith of the church is not exclusively directed to *the future* (in contrast to apocalyptic Judaism), but, rather, moves between the historical fulfilment of redemption in Christ and the expected ultimate revelation of Christ's victory in the future. The church lives in this tension. What she already holds firmly now in spite of the resistance of the faithless world will be fully disclosed before the church and the world in the days to come. Because the victory of God is the *victory* of the *Redeemer*, the end will not be the triumph of destruction and nothingness, but the *healing of the world.* John visualizes this end in a sequence of visions which are rooted in his view of redemptive history. These visions will be studied in the following chapters.

FROM THE PAROUSIA TO THE FINAL JUDGMENT

A. THE APPEARANCE OF CHRIST

The future of the church and the world is Jesus Christ. His appearance is certain and will be seen by all. That is the testimony of the entire New Testament. In Revelation, the church also awaits him and cries, 'Amen. Come, Kyrios Jesus' (22.20); but all those 'who pierced him' will be confronted by him, too. No one knows when the hour will come, not even the church. He will come like a thief (3.3; 16.15). The parousia is thus still one of God's secrets, the unveiling of which he has reserved to himself. Not only the date, but the entire event is shrouded in mystery. And yet the church already knows the One who is coming and, because this is so, her prophet is able to interpret the meaning of his coming in a vision.

I

Present-day interpretation of the Revelation of John is on the whole in agreement that Rev. 19.11-16 describes the return of Jesus Christ. But the individual features of the picture, and their significance for the theology of the book as a whole, in many respects still demand further consideration. The attempt will be made in the ensuing pages to understand the vision of the parousia within the framework of John's theological concepts. Scarcely another section of the book, in fact, is linked in such manifold ways with all others of its parts.

John sees the heavens opened (as in Ezek. 1.1), and Christ appears.[1] What takes place is portrayed according to a schema which is characteristic of John. First the white horse, which is the sign of Christ, appears, and then the *rider*. Just so, in 4.2, there appears first the throne, and then the one enthroned; and, in 14.14, first the white cloud, then the one who sits on it.[2] Horse, throne, and cloud, each say something essential about the one who sits on them; the throne is a symbol of dominion, the white cloud, of the parousia.[3] That Christ is here seen 'riding' on a white horse introduces a feature not to be found in any other early Christian portrayal of the parousia.[4] White is the colour of light, of heavenly beings, and of the eschatological,[5] while the horse is the mount used by kings and generals (v.16!). Christ thus appears as the eschatological ruler.[6]

What then follows is not really a description of the figure of the rider, but rather of his attributes and functions. In presenting these, the seer refers constantly to other passages in his book and, above all, to the Old Testament. This makes the entire picture somewhat abstract.[7] But what is at first even more puzzling is the peculiar and elaborate structure of the whole section. For one thing, it is to be observed that the description of Christ is suddenly interrupted by the introduction of the heavenly hosts in 19.14. Since no formal reason can be found for the insertion of this pictorial element between v.13 and v.15, we have to ask whether something in the content may supply the answer. It is striking, too (and something that has never been noticed, so far as I know), that the groups of statements which are separated by v.14 have been arranged with conscious intent by means of significant numbers.

The first group contains seven elements:
1. Christ is called 'faithful and true'.
2. He judges with justice and wages war.
3. His eyes are (like) a flame of fire.
4. On his head there are many diadems.
5. He bears a name that is written, which nobody knows but himself.
6. He is robed in a garment dipped in blood.
7. His name is called 'the Word of God'.
   The second group has four parts:
1. From his mouth there issues a sharp sword with which to smite the nations.
2. He will shepherd the nations with an iron rod.
3. He will tread the winepress of judgment.
4. On his robe and on his thigh there is written the name of the Omnipotent Ruler.

When one observes the structure of the text, one sees that this seemingly haphazard heaping together of formulae is actually ordered in an artistic manner and has meaning. Moreover, it is no longer perplexing that Christ should be named twice with two different names.[8] The first group concludes with the Logos name, the second with the title 'King of kings and Lord of lords'. We shall see that the first name is addressed to the church, which knows the revelation through the Word, while the second relates to the 'world' and its powers.[9] Indeed, all the assertions in both of the above groups point to this double significance of Christ's parousia. The two numbers, seven and four, are evidence precisely of that fact. For John, seven is especially the number of the fullness of the church, and of the Spirit.[10] Four is the traditional number of the cosmos, and of the earth.[11]

2

We shall begin with an investigation of the *first series* of characteristics of Christ.

1. Two statements appear, which resemble a name, and which are also to be found elsewhere in significant passages in Revelation: καλούμενος πιστὸς καὶ ἀληθινός.[12] In order to interpret these words, we have to start with 21.5 and 22.6, where πιστός and ἀληθινός are associated with the words of prophecy. No difference in their meaning is apparent, and they designate the promises of God which are recorded in Revelation as 'valid and trustworthy' — in contrast to words that are only empty promises and lies. The fact that the trustworthiness and validity of the prophecy has to be so strongly stressed implies the idea that the promise is completely unprovable. Its validity will be shown only in the future.[13] For the present, the promise can only be believed and 'held fast to, kept' against every temptation of those powers that seek to give it the lie (22.7; cf. 1.3; 12.17; 19.10; 20.4). Only the church of Jesus, which knows the author of the promises, is in a position to do this, for the author of the promises is God, who speaks to the church through Jesus Christ. For this reason 'the word of God' (1.2,9), or 'the words of prophecy' (1.3), is at the same time the μαρτυρία Ἰησοῦ Χριστοῦ.[14] The revelation of Jesus is many sided. It embraces the prophecy of the book which John had to

write,[15] but, in particular, personal words to the seven churches (chs.2-3) as well. Passages such as 6.9; 11.3; 12.17; 19.10 lead one to think of the prophetic proclamation of the gospel in general as a means of concretizing the eternal, joyful message which will be proclaimed by an angel in the end-time for the entire world (14.6).[16] The church's proclamation is viewed by John only under the prophetic aspect, in the sense that it is the actual proclamation of the word commissioned by God for the church and for the world in the special situation of the last days.

We have to go somewhat further afield in order to grasp the significance of the names of Christ in 19.11, and the lines by which they are connected with the notions of revelation found in the Apocalypse. When the words πιστὸς καὶ ἀληθινός are applied to Christ, they designate him as the one who is true to the word that he has given to his church. That John here reaches back to an Old Testament designation for God is clear from the introduction to the message to the church in Laodicea, where the two expressions are linked with the notion of witness, and stand in conscious contrast to the situation in that church (3.14). Laodicea is an unfaithful, dishonest church, which deceives itself with empty assertions (3.17). Her Lord will punish her, for he is the 'Amen, the faithful and true witness'. The divine name of Isa. 65.16 is here applied to Christ.[17] The formula ὁ μάρτυς ὁ πιστὸς καὶ ἀληθινός is nothing but a translation and explanation of the Hebrew word 'Amen'.[18] Because the formula πιστὸς καὶ ἀληθινός refers in Revelation to the word of promise, as we have seen, its association with ὁ μάρτυς becomes clear. The concept of witness adds no new element to the name of Christ. As the witness, Jesus reveals his μαρτυρία. He is the revealer whose word is backed by God. We saw that by μαρτυρία the Apocalypse always means the actual prophetic word of promise and assurance to the church of the last days. There is no reference here to 'the history of Christ'.[19] And there is no reason to understand the idea of witness in 1.5 in any other way. It does not speak of the death of Jesus, but of Christ as the revealer who provides his church with insight with regard to his Kingdom.[20]

Moreover, the title ὁ πρωτότοκος τῶν νεκρῶν, which follows in 1.5, is not (as so often asserted) merely the second part of the kerygmatic formula, 'dead, risen, exalted',[21] and T. Holtz has correctly shown that the title 'not only gives expression to the resurrection itself', but at the same time to the promise of the redemption of the dead.[22] The formula embraces both: Christ was himself a dead man who, however, is now alive (1.18), and who has become a promise to all who are dead. In 1.5 there is added to the title of the redeemer and the eschatological revealer, whose word is characterized as ever valid, that of the Lord of all the powers of the world.

Our investigation has shown that the Christ who is to return is, in 19.11, first of all characterized as the one who is *devoted to his church*, who will keep the word that he has given her and show that it was no empty promise.

2. It is with good reason that Holtz has argued that the second characteristic of Christ in 19.11 also describes 'his relationship to his church'.[23] When he comes to prove the truth of his word, he will appear as *judge of the church*. 'He judges in righteousness' is an expression for his redeeming 'act of' judgment, in accordance with Isa. 11.4a.[24] He procures justice for his church. John shows what that means for the church through the image of the thousand-year kingdom (20.4-6). But at the same time 'he wages war'. πολεμεῖν is used of Christ only one other time (2.16), and here too in the sense of his judging his church.[25] He sits in judgment over the sham members of his church who bring trouble on the true church (cf. 2.2f., 14f., 20-25).

3. The two following elements in the picture are likewise not merely in a general way parts of the 'portrayal of Christ as he appears to the seer as the one who comes again',[26] but are closely linked with the first. We find the *'eyes* (like) a flame of fire' in the vision that depicts Jesus as the Lord of the church.[27] In the message to the church in Thyatira (2.18) these eyes are likewise directed at the church, and they 'see through' its situation.[28]

4. The 'many *diadems*' (19.12) seemingly constitute an exception, and one would be inclined to expect them after v.14. Nevertheless, this symbol of unlimited power is related in manifold ways to 13.1 (cf. also 12.4), and is a facet of the theme of the Satanic powers as antitypes over against God and his Christ, which characterizes the entire Book of Revelation.[29]

Their power is represented by seven (or ten) diadems.[30] The target of the attack of the dragon, and above all of the Antichrist, is the church of Jesus. It is even given to the Antichrist 'to wage war against the saints and to conquer them' (13.17). But over against this sinister threat the church is told in the parousia vision that Christ will show himself to be the Lord of the church, infinitely superior in power, so that she may trust him even while she perishes. Thus it is precisely through this emphasis upon the lordship of him who is to come that his devotion to his church is revealed.

5. The *name* that no one except he himself knows perhaps also belongs to the same theme,[31] for in the description of the Antichrist as we find it in 13.1, 'blasphemous names' (or 'a blasphemous name') follow the mention of the diadems.[32] According to the ancient's way of thinking, the name reveals the nature of its bearer.[33] It is the nature of the Antichrist to blaspheme God. Christ in his parousia bears a name that reveals his mystery, a name which as yet no one knows, and which John therefore cannot read. The church, too, in this present age still stands before the *mystery of Christ,* although she already knows him and may call him by various names. But in his parousia the very depths of his nature will be revealed to the church through his new name.

It is therefore pointless to seek in the secret name one that is already known, for no conceivable word could possibly express the reality that will be revealed only in the parousia.[34] The closest parallel is undoubtedly I John 3.2, where hope is expressed for the revelation of the secret nature of Christ ('we shall see him as he is'), and also of the church ('it is not yet apparent what we shall be . . . we shall be like him'; cf. Rev. 2.17).

6. Now this conception of the parousia sheds new light on the difficult statement about Christ's garment, which is dipped in blood. This image is today almost unanimously explained with reference to Isa. 63.2-3:

Why is thy apparel red,
    and thy garments like his that treads in the wine press?

I have trodden the wine press alone,

and from the peoples no one was with me;
I trod them in my anger
and trampled them in my wrath;
their life blood is sprinkled upon my garments,
and I have stained all my raiment.

But this interpretation is not at all well founded. For one thing, mention of the one who treads the winepress appears only as the third element of the *second* part of the passage (19.15), as an image of judgment upon the nations (as in 14.20). And so far there has been no mention whatever of any battle. Christ already wears his bloody garment as he comes from heaven.[35]

The blood which John repeatedly mentions in connection with the *church* is *the blood of Christ himself*, who is the slain lamb.[36] His 'blood', not as a physical substance, but as a metaphorical expression for his self-sacrifice, procures forgiveness and is the sign of his total victory which the church already shares (5.5,9; cf. 1.5; 7.14; 12.10). He who comes thus wears the sign of the lamb that has been sacrificed, the garment dipped in his own blood.[37] This interpretation is the only one that at the same time does justice to the obviously more difficult variant reading $\beta\epsilon\beta\alpha\mu\mu\acute{\epsilon}\nu o\nu$.[38] The 'dipping' of the garment in blood has nothing to do with the imagery of Isa. 63.1-4. But it is clear that from a very early period Rev. 19.13 was no longer understood in its relationship to the church, but was assimilated to the Old Testament picture, which is taken up in 19.15. It was this that led to the old and well-attested variant reading $\pi\epsilon\rho\iota\rho\epsilon\rho\alpha\mu\mu\acute{\epsilon}\nu o\nu$.[39]

The garment of the coming Christ thus reveals the truth and the reality of his redemption in its eternal validity for the church.

7. Closely related to this is the *name,* which is mentioned in conclusion: $\acute{o}\ \lambda\acute{o}\gamma o\varsigma\ \tau o\tilde{v}\ \theta\epsilon o\tilde{v}$. In attempting to interpret this we ought not too hastily to refer to John 1.1. The presuppositions for calling Jesus by the Logos title are to be found in the theology of Revelation itself.

First of all, it is important to note the perfect $\kappa\acute{\epsilon}\kappa\lambda\eta\tau\alpha\iota$, which is so unusual in this context. We would expect the present (cf. 19.1; 1.9; 11.8; 12.9; 16.16). We have, therefore, to assume that some particular purpose underlies the use of the perfect and, in fact, in the light of the context this unexpected form takes on a special significance. It points back to the time of the church from the standpoint of the parousia. Jesus is once and for all given to the church as the Word of God. In him she had the revelation of God at all times. He not only bore witness to the Word, but was the Word in person. For this reason, the prophecy which John received from Jesus has to do not merely with his Word, but with his whole history: his birth, death, exaltation and coming again.[40] And so it is that his church holds fast not only to 'the testimony of Jesus', but also to his name, that is to say, to Jesus himself (2.13), or to 'faith in Jesus' (2.13; 14.12).

The distinguishing mark of the revelation given to the church as 'Word' is the fact that it includes the admission that its truth is both provisional and unprovable. The Word is therefore continually attacked, and liable to attack, from within and from without. This is why there comes the constant admonition to 'keep' it.

In Christ's parousia unyielding faith will be gloriously vindicated, and 'the Word' will be attested as the truth, for 'the Word of God' will appear before the eyes of the church and the world in the person of the victorious Lord.

Thus all these terms describing the nature and the function of the Coming One stand in an inner relationship to one another and reveal him as the hope long awaited by the church, to which he will turn first of all in his parousia.[41]

It is wrong to see in the picture of the parousia in Revelation only the judge as depicted by Michelangelo! Jesus is first and above all viewed as the unveiling of the grace from which the church already lives in the midst of all her temptations.[42]

3

But now, with 19.14, the portrayal of the coming Christ is interrupted, and the mighty entourage of the heavenly hosts is introduced. John is undoubtedly thinking of angelic armies, such as were expected in Jewish and Christian eschatology (Test. Levi 3.3; 1QM 12.1-5; 19.1; Mark 13.27; Matt. 25.31; II Thess. 1.7f.).

In the following verses, along with a second series of his personal characteristics, the significance of the Coming One *for the nations* comes into focus. *Vis à vis* the nations, he is the judge, the nature of whose activity is suggested by means of three words taken from the Old Testament.

1. In the first of these John connects Isa. 49.2 with Isa. 11.4b.[43] Christ will judge with a *sword* issuing from his mouth (his Word). 2. The words from Ps. 2.9, 'He will pasture them with a rod of iron', allude to the same judgment.[44] 3. The third Old Testament picture, that of the winepress (Isa. 63.3; similarly, Joel 4.13), also appears in Rev. 14.19f., but in 19.15 it is connected with the metaphor of the wine of God's wrath.[45] 4. Finally, the name is pronounced: 'King of kings and Lord of lords'. Once again John is referring to the Old Testament, where God is called 'the God of gods and the Lord of lords'.[46] The name intimates that Christ will appear in divine omnipotence.[47]

The execution of this judgment in 19.17-21 — that is, the public manifestation of what the true situation is with regard to power and justice — is placed entirely within the framework of what has become evident from 19.15f. about the significance of Christ for the world.

As a prelude to the drama, and even before the armies of the enemy come in sight (19.17f.), an angel assembles all the carrion birds for the horrible 'meal of God', as in the prophecy of Gog in Ezek. 39, for this judgment aims above all at the unveiling of Jesus' triumph over the Antichrist, who appears in the likeness of Gog also in 6.1f.[48] The Antichrist and his false prophet are then presented in an amazing powerlessness. In spite of the enormous massing of all the enemy's forces (19.19; the same thing is described in 16.12-16), they have only to be 'seized' and 'thrown' into the lake of fire (19.20). And their followers fall before the word of Christ (19.21). No trace of any battle! An angel can arrest the satanic dragon and render him harmless for the time of the church's triumph, the hidden nature of which has been revealed in the resurrection (20.4-6).[49] Even his last rebellion after his liberation serves only 'one purpose': to reveal his powerlessness (20.7-10).

A decisive feature in this picture of the parousia is that John never gives up his central christological conception. For him there is only *one battle* and victory of Christ, which already lies in the past. With his birth into this world, his death and his exaltation, he hurled the dragon from his place in heaven and enabled his church to win the victory (12.5,10f.). As the slain lamb he has become 'the lion of Judah' who is everywhere victorious (ἐνίκησεν), and into whose hands dominion over the world has been committed (5.5).[50] John knows nothing of any other battle or victory of Christ. Since the issue has already been decided in the death of Jesus, the eschatological war, for which God's enemies prepare, will not take place.[51]

There is only one passage in the entire book of Revelation which would seem to contradict this view of the matter, and which therefore requires further discussion: 17.9b-17. There are several reasons for regarding this passage as a later interpolation.[52] We find here a calculation of the last days after the manner of Jewish apocalyptic which is otherwise completely foreign to the book of Revelation. It is very probable that the author of this interpolation wrote at the time of Domitian, and sought to characterize his time as the last epoch of history, and the reigning emperor as Antichrist and Nero *redivivus*.

This redactor then gives his portrayal of the parousia (17.12-14). He clearly borrows from 19.11-16, but he diverges from it in a significant way. The same situation is described: the beast together with the kings who serve him is prepared for war (17.14; cf. 19.19). Corresponding to the redactor's interpretation of the beast's ten horns, ten kings appear here in place of 'the kings of the earth', who throughout the book represent 'collectively' all the political powers on earth.[53] Now, however, the redactor speaks of a battle or a victory of the Lamb which is based upon the lordship of the Lamb (whereas in 5.5 the victory is the precondition of his lordship). Following this, the armies of 19.14 are interpreted as the church, with the use of three expressions that occur only here in Revelation: κλητοὶ καὶ ἐκλεκτοὶ καὶ πιστοί (in the sense of 'believers'). It is, therefore, evident (leaving other reasons aside) that 17.12-14 is a portrayal of the parousia which was inserted into the text at a later date, which knew and made use of individual elements from 19.11ff., but which failed to maintain the clear christological conception characteristic of John.

In his description of the parousia, John, as we saw, opens up no fantastic, speculative dreams, but rather his own belief in the final fulfilment of all promises in Christ. Christ will bring the full disclosure of the realities which are already known to the church through faith, of the true nature of Jesus, and of his victory over all powers, powers which are still at the present able to develop their brutal and devastating force and impose it upon the entire world, but which the church recognizes in their ultimate powerlessness and, for that reason, refuses either to deify them or worship them in spite of all tribulations. He Who Comes will vindicate the faith of the church and reveal himself as redeemer, judge, and lord. Thus the proclamation of the coming Christ becomes a message for the present, strengthening the church in all temptations, and calling both church and world to repentance, for both must await the encounter with him.[54]

B. THE REVELATION OF THE REDEEMED
AND THE UNREDEEMED

Charles calls Rev. 20 'a constant source of unsurmountable difficulty to the exegete', and can see no way to solve the problem save through a rearrangement of the final sections of the book.[55] Indeed, he finds this chaotic disorder in the concluding part of Revelation all the more surprising in that he finds elsewhere 'a structural unity and a steady development of thought from the first chapter to the close of 20.3'.[56] We have to consider this problem further and to ask whether a clear development of thought is not after all to be found in the order of the text as it now lies before us, and what considerations may have moved the apocalyptist in ch. 20 to take over these concepts saturated by tradition.

1

Aside from the reasons already adduced by Charles, many exegetes have been surprised by the peculiar provisionary elimination of Satan, by the concept of the millennium, which is not to be found elsewhere in the New Testament, by the idea of a further, final liberation of Satan, and by the introduction of the nations Gog and Magog, whose very existence seems rather surprising after 19.21. In recent discussion some have sought to overcome the difficulty by assuming that John, desiring to present the apocalyptic picture in its entirety, has worked these elements of the tradition into his book in spite of the fact that they really contradict his own conception of the matter.[57]

On the other hand we must ask the question: Is there perhaps in the framework of John's eschatology a basic motif that might explain the peculiar character and the strangeness of this whole cycle of visions from the parousia to the final judgment? I have shown in the first section of this study that all the statements about Jesus' appearance (19.11-16) give manifold expression to a single basic motif: *the Coming One is He who has already come, who has already altered the world's total situation*, who has overcome all powers and principalities, who is already known in the faith of his church as Revealer, Redeemer, and Lord of all lords, who now steps from the twilight of the unprovable and the unavailable into the radiant light of unveiled existence and vindicates the faith of his church. For John, what the future will bring is the unveiling of the reality already created in the history of Jesus.[58]

2

Precisely the same motif, it seems to me, dominates the whole of chapter 20. Many interpreters have been struck by the fact that we have to do here with at least an apparent repetition of the situation already observed in 19.11-21. That is the main reason that gave rise to the profoundly influential interpretation of the millennial kingdom as the time of the church.[59] And there are for that reason among the arguments in its favour some points that are well worthy of consideration, for the whole image in certain ways agrees strangely with the portrayal of the end-history (between the first and second coming of Jesus).

(a) The defeat of the dragon is reported not only in 20.1-3, but also earlier in 12.7-9. The repetition of the interpretation of the dragon as 'the ancient serpent, the Devil and Satan' (20.2) is a direct reference to 12.9!

(b) Rev. 20.4-6 speaks of the church of God.[60] Two groups are distinguished, as is also the case elsewhere in Revelation. First of all, John sees the martyrs who have been beheaded because of their witness to Jesus and the word of God. A quite similar description is to be found in 6.9.

With $\kappa\alpha\grave{\iota}\,o\check{\iota}\tau\iota\nu\epsilon\varsigma$ a second group is introduced, those who had worshipped neither the beast nor his image, and who had not received the mark of the Antichrist on their foreheads. The church is also described in this way in 13.8, 15-17; 15.2.[61] Here she is seen sitting upon thrones and ruling, which reminds us of the fact that, according to Exod. 19.6 (cf. 1.6,9; 5.10), as the church of the end-time she is already $\beta\alpha\sigma\iota\lambda\epsilon\acute{\iota}\alpha$. The juxtaposition of the words $\beta\alpha\sigma\iota\lambda\epsilon\acute{\iota}\alpha$ and $\iota\epsilon\rho\epsilon\tilde{\iota}\varsigma$ makes it probable that John here ascribes to the church royal dignity.[62] 'They shall rule' over the earth (5.10)[63] — precisely as those who suffer under the yoke of the world powers! And when, in 20.4, they receive the promise of the resurrection, we are reminded of the fact that the true life has already been bestowed on them during the end-time (3.1; 22.17). Even the priesthood is a part of their honour long before the parousia (20.4; 1.6; 5.10; according to Exod. 19.6; Isa. 61.6).

(c) Finally, 20.7-10 also appears to be a repetition of the church's situation in the end-time. She groans under the persecution of Satan and his creatures, the persecution that becomes ever more intense as the end draws nearer (11.7; 12.13,17; 13.7,16f.; 16.12ff.). Nevertheless, the church's victory has already been assured through the advent of Jesus in the past (12.10f.).

This striking parallelism must have been intended, and it must have its special significance within the framework of John's theology. In order to understand it rightly, we have at the same time to observe that, in spite of all points of agreement, we are not dealing with a mere recapitulation, but that all common traits appear in a *completely altered context*.

3

The final appearance of Christ precedes the whole cycle of visions (19.11ff.). His appearance has changed the dragon's situation fundamentally. After his fall from heaven (12.10f.) the dragon has lost his rights as accuser of his brethren because of the historical intervention of Christ. But there is still some time left to him to continue his evil work. But his term comes to an end with the parousia of Christ. He is seized, thrown into chains, and cast into the underworld, which is then shut and sealed so that he is no longer able to deceive anyone.

The seer here employs concepts which play a significant role in many ancient Oriental myths regarding the underworld. The terminology itself has a relationship to that of the story of the descent of Ishtar into the underworld, where she is 'shut up'. Bel-Marduk, too, is 'held captive there, guarded, shut up in prison'.[64] Parseeism likewise knows of the chaining of the serpent Azi-Dahaka.[65]

We are not, of course, to suppose that John was directly influenced by heathen myths, for the Old Testament had already taken over certain of these motifs. Thus the realm of the dead is understood as a prison in Ps. 18.6; 116.3 (cf. Acts 2.24; I Peter 3.18).[66] And Isa. 24.22 speaks of the imprisonment of the hosts in the heaven and of the kings of the earth in the pit:

> They will be gathered together
>   as prisoners in a pit;
> They will be shut up in a prison,
>   and after many days they will be punished.

Here, too, the underworld is a prison where the enemies of God are kept temporarily until the Day of Judgment.[67]

The basic motif that shapes the entire series of visions from the parousia to the final judgment clearly shows what distinguishes this image of God's victory over the dragon from ch.12. The apparent power of the dragon, which has already been overcome by Jesus' historical victory, but which is still dangerous for those who do not believe in Christ, has now 'objectively' — that is, in a manner recognizable by the world as well — ceased to exist.[68] This conception carries with it a paraenetic element for the church: she should never at any time bow to this apparent power before the consummation. We shall see that the brief release allowed to the dragon is to be understood in the light of the same basic motif.[69]

4

The sealing up of Satan for a thousand years provides in advance the link between the first vision and that of the millennial kingdom (20.4-6). As we have seen, this vision too is linked with the portrayal of the church of the end-time by a whole series of statements,[70] so much so that O. Cullmann can observe that 'the phase following the parousia represents only a significant recapitulation of the one that goes before'.[71]

But, once again, the situation of the church appears here in a new light. What surpasses the state of affairs in the time before the parousia is the breaking in of eternal life into the whole of human existence through the resurrection.[72] The life which had already been appropriated by the church in faith now becomes manifest. In like manner, the characteristics and functions that had already in secret crowned the eschatological existence of the church also become fully and completely manifest: the members of the church are the rulers of the world, together with Christ their Lord.[73] In the millennial kingdom their *secret nature will thus be revealed*. It is to be noticed that the seer speaks here not only of a reversal of the former circumstances so that the church — once a slave of all kinds of earthly powers — becomes itself an eschatological slaveholder. John is not concerned with the triumph of the believers over the unbelievers (although desired by the church time and again!), but rather with the revelation of the *'king-ship'* of believers in the sense of an evidence of their absolute *freedom* from all human and superhuman forces. John has therefore omitted any mention of an object of their rule.[74]

In like manner, their *priesthood* now shines forth in its full glory. To be sure, it is not altogether obvious why the notion of priesthood should appear in this passage. John speaks of the priesthood only in connection with Exod. 19.6 ('and you shall be to me a kingdom of priests and a holy nation'; cf. also Isa. 61.6), which he quotes, and he never implies any concrete priestly action on the part of the church. The idea of a mis-sionary activity, which could be connected with it,[75] recedes altogether into the background as a result of the subject matter of the book.[76] Charles finds it surprising 'that the preaching of the gospel during the millennium will only in part be successful, though the active impersonations of evil have been wholly removed from the earth for this period'.[77] But in fact, John speaks neither of evangelization nor, indeed, of so much as one single convert aside from 'the peoples from the four corners of the earth'. Indeed, the conclusion of the parousia vision (19.21) suggests that he intends to speak of the death of all unbelievers, and that any notion of the resurrected and the non-resurrected ones standing side by side in the millennium is completely foreign to him. So, too, in the vision of the Last Judgment, only the dead appear, that is to say, the enemies of God.

The words ἱερεῖς τοῦ θεοῦ refer to the redeemed, not with regard to their activity, but with regard to their *nature*. Their entire existence is a priesthood, in the sense that it is a sign of their 'having been ransomed from among mankind' through the blood of Jesus (1.5; 5.9f.; 14.3f.), a sign (for the world) of election out of the world, a promise of God's grace for all in the midst of the night of judgment.[78] In their midst redemption is being consummated, and for this reason the entire church in reality occupies a priestly position between man and God.

But the church can demonstrate the reality neither of her kingship nor of her priesthood during the time of her pilgrimage. Only the great moment of Christ's revelation will bring what she really is to light. The fact, however, that she remains a *sign* of the promise even in the moment of Christ's triumph means that the church is not herself the goal of all the ways and promises of God.

Thus, here too, the basic motif of the unveiling of the hidden realities of faith discloses the meaning of the vision. In the light of this motif it becomes understandable why the seer still expects this revelation to be given to *the old world*, the world of faith. In this context the number 1000 has lost its temporal significance, as have all numbers in the apocalypse that denote a specific 'time', and has become an expression for the peculiar character of the time that is intended by the concept. Here it is the time of the revealed Messiah.[79]

5

Rev. 20.7-10 is the most difficult section of all. Already at the end of v.3 a second liberation of Satan was indicated as a part of God's plan in history. This is now described. We have already called attention to the parallelism between this section and the situation of the church in the end-time. And, once again, the vision is shaped by the *same basic motif* that was at work throughout ch.20, for the final liberation of Satan serves only one purpose: the final and total unveiling of his nature, of the defeat he had experienced long ago, of his powerlessness and perdition.

The nature of Satan is the radical negation of God and his church. Thus there appears the grotesque idea of preparations for war and the mustering of armies against the community of those who are already resurrected to indestructible eternal life. Their eschatological life can never be taken from them; they are completely unreachable by all the powers of Hell, even the second death, which is identified with the lake of fire, the place of the damned.[80]

The allusions to the armies of Satan, specifically to 'the nations from the four corners of the earth, *Gog and Magog*', are extremely obscure. Who are they? The collapse of the enemies of Christ, to whom all belong who are not members of his church (13.8), according to 19.21 brought them death through the word of Christ. Thus at the time of the millennium there are no people living on the old earth other than the resurrected ones; otherwise one would have to assume that John was thinking of 'neutral' nations which did not openly join the armies of the Antichrist. But that would contradict the unqualified statements of 19.11-21, as well as the sharp separation throughout the entire book between the people in the world and the church. The conjecture that John has somewhat unfortunately taken over traditions which were not fully in harmony with his own conceptions, and which he could not incorporate without inconsistency,[81] is also very unlikely, for he elsewhere shows that he knew how to work with traditions and to shape them in a clear and masterly manner.

Another interpretation seems to me more appropriate. The vision of the chaining of Satan, which is especially closely linked by v.3 and the introductory words of v.7 with the vision of 20.7-10, leads us into a well-defined conceptual world. It deals with the kingdom of the demonic powers and of the dead as the prison in the underworld. According to the complex ancient oriental and biblical apprehension of the matter, this underworld manifests itself not only in the grave, in the depths, or in the ocean,[82] but quite generally in all areas which are separated from life, in the desert or in lonely, far-away places of the earth.[83] 'The Tammuz who has vanished into the realm of the dead is called (CT, XV, 26) the remote one. Perhaps Ps. 61.3, where the individual calls for help *miqqēṣē hāʾāreṣ*, from the end of the earth, also refers to the realm of the dead.'[84] The psalm indicates that the entrance to the underworld was thought to lie on the fringes of the earth. The great ocean, which in Rev. 20.13 is an expression for the world of the dead, also begins there.[85] The expression of the apocalypse, 'the four corners of the earth', likewise points to the earth's remotest fringes. These limits of the sphere of life stand in contrast to the middle of the world, τὸ πλάτος τῆς γῆς, which is the place of the church of the millennium.[86] These contexts are of decisive importance for the understanding of John's way of expressing himself. Thus vv.7-10 are to be interpreted as follows: Satan entices the ghostly nations of the dead, and the demons, 'innumerable as the sand of the sea', from the four corners of the earth where the underworld manifests itself, in order to make war on the resurrected ones.[87] The mythical names Gog and Magog are also quite fitting in this context, since they do not allude here to historical nations, but to the bands of Hell, similar to the armies of Abaddon which ascend from the bowels of the earth (9.1-11), or to the hordes of demons in 9.13-19 (note here also the cosmic number 4!).[88] Thus at the end there comes the revelation of the unredeemed and their aims (namely, the destruction of the church). But the church is indestructible, and now, even 'physically' so. Because Christ has long since won the victory over all powers, no fresh battle takes place,[89] but rather a fire from heaven consumes the whole ghostly array, and Satan is delivered over to the lake of fire where the Antichrist and his helper already are. And so, once again, in this section too, we find exactly the same basic motif.

6

The whole cycle of visions introduced by the appearance of Christ is concluded with the Last Judgment. The judgment is executed by God himself, who appears on the great white throne bearing the colour of heaven and of the eschaton.[90] The old world is doomed to dissolution, once it has seen the triumph of Christ and his people.[91] Death, which already appears in the Old Testament, as it does in the Revelation of John, under the double aspect of 'power' and of 'space', yields up all his dead.[92] Since, according to 20.4-6, the first resurrection has already brought God's church to eternal life, one must assume that the seer is here thinking exclusively of those whose names are not written in the book of life, which is the book of the Lamb (13.18). The ἔργα are, therefore, in all likelihood to be understood only in the negative sense as *sinful 'works'* and the 'books' as *registers of sins*.[93] At any rate, John makes clear that 'works cannot save us'. He does not allow us to place our hope on our deeds. 'If someone was not found in the book of life, he was thrown into the lake of fire' (20.15). Verse 15 does not indicate that some names of the dead will be found in the book of life; it rather indicates that *the only criterion of salvation* is the fact that our name is written in the book of life. The decisive criterion in the universal judgment is that of belonging to Christ, which is represented through the image of

the book of life of the Lamb, who has procured forgiveness
through his sacrificial death (1.5; 7.14).[94] But because it is only
the sentence passed upon the enemies of God that is in question
here, the judgment takes on a completely negative character
(20.15). This peculiar feature, once again, can be explained
only in the light of the same basic motif which we have
encountered over and over again in ch.20. Everything has really
already been decided in the historical decision of Jesus and in
the decision of men with regard to him. The judgment therefore can be nothing else than the universal *unveiling* of
decisions that have already been made. Since the redeemed are
already resurrected, they are exempt from final judgment of
the world. Thus we find here a conception that is related to the
Gospel of John in the profoundest way: whoever believes in
Jesus will not be judged; whoever does not believe is judged
already, because he has not believed in the name of the only
Son of God (John 3.18f.).[95]

7

Our study has shown that a single guiding motif lies behind the
whole cycle of visions from the parousia to the final judgment
which makes clear John's true interest in the traditionary
material drawn from the Old Testament and later Judaism. For
the seer the entire future has already been decided in the
history of Jesus Christ. From it, the church already lives in the
end-time, albeit this is still hidden, unprovable, and although
she is herself still subject to temptation. With the events that
will accompany the future appearance of Jesus, the truth of the
realities in which the church has believed will be made evident
to the entire world.

But, on the other hand, we must consider that the completion of what has already been realized in Jesus' historical
deed is present only and exclusively in his person, and is only
true in the church because Jesus lives in her midst and because
she remains gathered about him as his people (1.12ff.; 14.1-5).
The future remains concealed in the church's existence and in
her history, for at the present time not only the world, but also
the church, is shaken by tears, suffering, lamentation, pain, and
even the threat of death (21.4). The church therefore awaits a
new revelation of Jesus in which her weakness and her liability

to temptation will be transformed into pure glory. This revelation is not merely, as it were, like the pulling away of a curtain from a covered monument, but *a new creative act of God*, the consummation of the judgment and of the resurrection, the impingement of the invisible upon the visible, physical world.

Revelation 20 is not concerned to present a somewhat abstruse, private teaching of a speculative apocalyptist, but the same message, seen in vision, as that proclaimed by the other witnesses of the New Testament, that salvation both for the present and for the future lies in Jesus Christ alone, and that the future will be the fulfilment of all the promises received in Jesus through faith.

The final visions, the images of the new Jerusalem, deal with this new world of fulfilment.

II

THE NEW JERUSALEM

Rich in imagery as the Book of Revelation is, one of its most spectacular imaginative creations is the portrayal of the holy city, Jerusalem, which, after the consummation of world history, descends from heaven linking heaven and earth. As the light-flooded picture of the presence of God among men, it has aroused the longings of godly poets and painters, and has through the centuries exerted a decisive influence on the shape of Christian church buildings. Recent investigations have shown that the basic idea which influenced the form of the medieval cathedral down to the smallest details was that of the earthly copy of the glorious heavenly city.[96] The artists of the Middle Ages sought to fashion their churches precisely according to John's vision of the heavenly city, so as to create a visible image of the nature of the church.

This theology in stone and glass, light and colour, in the keenest anticipation of the future, interprets the nature of the church as man's heavenly home into which he may even now in the present enter.[97]

Fascinating as the unearthly splendour of this exaltation of the church may be, it unquestionably did violence both to the express statements and to the intentions of John, for he understands the holy city as an entity which belongs only to the future, and which presupposes the coming of Christ in glory and the complete consummation of his victory.[98]

John's heavenly city which comes down to earth is, however, really not the original source of inspiration for this conception of the church, but rather similar New Testament pictorial words which speak of a heavenly city to which the church of

Jesus already belongs. Through a theological interweaving of such concepts with Rev. 21 a wonderful visual concretization was nevertheless arrived at, which could be taken over not only for works of art such as paintings, but also for the earthly 'habitation' of the church in which its services of worship were conducted – and which confirmed its self-understanding.

We shall discuss the relationship of the New Testament passages in question to the Revelation of John. In Galatians, Paul speaks of the 'Jerusalem above' which is 'our mother', and places it over against 'the present Jerusalem' (Gal. 4.25-31). In doing this, Paul takes up a concept already present in Jewish tradition, that of a new Jerusalem, in order to describe the church's peculiar situation within salvation history with relation to that of Judaism. Without going into this passage more closely, we would note the strange coincidence of a temporal and a spatial designation of the city ($\nu\tilde{\nu}\nu=\mathring{\alpha}\nu\omega$, vv.25f.). Without doubt, the heavenly Jerusalem is for Paul 'the new aeon'.[99]

But the new aeon is through the eschatological Christ-event already *present* in the church of Jesus 'in the anticipation of the eschaton peculiar to the Christian faith'.[100] And yet, the anticipation of the end which is experienced in the church retains its character as promise, for the church is not made one with the heavenly Jerusalem. Rather, the heavenly city is called the origin of the church, 'her mother'. P. Bonnard has formulated the relationship between the two entities very well: 'The church militant announces (and not only by words, but by her life) the heavenly Jerusalem . . . Paul affirms that believers, members of the church, are "sons" of the Kingdom which alone is the "mother".'[101] Out of this heavenly kingdom of which the church is already a part, Christ will appear as Saviour.

The situation is in no way different when the Epistle to the Hebrews takes up the image of the heavenly city for which Abraham looked, which has 'firm foundations, whose builder and maker is God' (Heb. 11.10). The church has already 'come' to 'this heavenly reality', and yet it remains even for the believers of the new covenant 'the future city', the city for which 'we seek' (13.14).[102] Thus there is in the concept of the New Jerusalem, both with Paul and the author of Hebrews, a peculiar relationship of tension, in which the church must live.

A. JERUSALEM IN THE OLD TESTAMENT AND IN LATER JUDAISM

1

The two New Testament books just mentioned, and also the Revelation of John, speak of this city as an entity that is well known, the origin of which requires not the least explanation. Knowledge of it in the Christian church is presupposed, which suggests that the traditions were widespread. We will, therefore, as briefly as possible, seek to trace the history of this conception.

Our texts refer us to the Old Testament. But they cannot be understood without a knowledge of the development of the Old Testament's concepts of hope in later Judaism. We shall, therefore, first of all attempt to sketch the Old Testament's presuppositions and the manner in which they evolved in later Judaism.

The history of the Jerusalem-hope is a most unusual one and can only be understood in the light of the Israelite experience of God. The city of Jerusalem, when it first emerged into the light of history, possessed no natural advantages that might give promise of its future significance, indeed veneration.

Located in a not easily accessible spot in the Judaean mountains (c.800 metres above sea level, more than 1000 metres above the Jordan valley), and not at a natural intersection of important trade routes, the Jebusite settlement was not particularly attractive even to the Israelites. 'It is not to nature that Jerusalem owes its pre-eminent position in present-day Palestine; that Jerusalem has become what it is in our day is because history has made it so, in spite of nature.'[103]

Until the days of David, the city meant nothing to the *faith* of the Israelite tribes.[104] But, since it was centrally located and on neutral ground between Judah and the northern tribes, the king saw in it the ideal place to establish his residence. The transfer of the Ark of the Covenant to the new capital city gave to Jerusalem importance and glory as the place of God's presence, and the building of the temple put the seal on its significance. With surprising speed, belief in the promise of God to the Davidides, and in the presence of God, was linked

unbreakably with the city, so that Jerusalem as a royal city and
a religious symbol survived not only the collapse of the united
monarchy, but all the catastrophes that were to follow, even
the loss of the sacred Ark and the temple. The holy city,[105] or
the holy mountain of Yahweh,[106] as the visible symbol which in
itself embraces God's presence among his people, became the
bearer of all expectations for the future and, as such, the sign of
God's faithfulness to his chosen people!

2

Later hopes were kindled above all by the books of Isaiah and
Ezekiel. We quote the most important texts.

In Isaiah 2.1-4 Jerusalem appears in connection with the
motif of the eschatological pilgrimage of the nations to Zion:

> The word which Isaiah the son of Amoz saw concerning
> Judah and Jerusalem:
>> In days to come the mountain of the house of the Lord
>> shall be established as the highest of the mountains,
>>> and shall be raised above the hills;
>> and all the nations shall flow to it,
>>> and many peoples shall come and say:
>> 'Come, let us go up to the mountain of the Lord,
>>> to the house of the God of Jacob;
>> that he may teach us his ways
>>> and that we may walk in his paths.'
>> For out of Zion shall go forth the law,
>>> and the word of the Lord from Jerusalem.
>> He shall judge between the nations,
>>> and shall decide for many peoples;
>> and they shall beat their swords into ploughshares,
>>> and their spears into pruning hooks;
>> nation shall not lift up sword against nation,
>>> neither shall they learn war any more.

'The place to which Yahweh has bound his salvation will rise
out of its lowly and unknown state and will be seen by all the
world in its *doxa*.'[107] The same motifs appear yet again in the
mighty picture in Isa. 60. The new Jerusalem will be the centre
of the world; above it Yahweh's shining glory will radiate, and
all the nations will rejoice in its light. Innumerable multitudes

of kings and peoples will come as pilgrims to the holy city.[108]

> Your gates shall be open continually;
>   day and night they shall not be shut;
> that through them may be brought the wealth of the nations,
>   with their kings led in procession. . . .
>
> The sons of those who oppressed you
>   shall come bending low to you;
> and all who despised you
>   shall bow down at your feet;
> they shall call you the City of the Lord,
>   the Zion of the Holy One of Israel. (Isa. 60.11-14)

Then Jerusalem will finally become the place of continual encounter with God:

> The sun shall be no more your light by day,
> nor for brightness shall the moon
>   give light to you by night;
> but the Lord will be your everlasting light,
>   and your God will be your glory. (Isa. 60.19)

The citizens of the city will all be 'just',

> Your people shall all be righteous;
>   they shall possess the land for ever,
> the shoot of my planting, the work of my hands,
>   that I may be glorified. (Isa. 60.21; cf. Isa. 54.13)

and Jerusalem will be called the 'city of Yahweh', the 'Zion of the Holy One of Israel':

> They shall call you the City of the Lord,
>   the Zion of the Holy One of Israel. (Isa. 60.14)

Isaiah 54.11-14 depicts the glory of the Jerusalem of the future in radiant colours. Her husband, the Redeemer, will with renewed mercy once again call back his 'barren', 'forsaken', 'rejected wife' (Isa. 54.6). The faithfulness of God to the people he had once chosen will be manifested triumphantly in the eschatological renewal of the covenant.

> For the mountains may depart

> and the hills be removed,
> but my steadfast love shall not depart from you,
> and my covenant of peace shall not be removed. (Isa. 54.10)

The new Jerusalem will be an earthly construction, but it will have about it the transcendent beauty of a city of sparkling precious stones:[109]

> O afflicted one, storm-tossed, and not comforted,
> behold, I will set your stones in antimony,
> and lay your foundations with sapphires.

> I will make your pinnacles of agate,
> your gates of carbuncles,
> and all your walls of precious stones.

> All your sons shall be taught by the Lord
> and great shall be the prosperity of your sons.

> In righteousness you shall be established;
> you shall be far from oppression,
> for you shall not fear;
> and from terror, for it shall not come near you. (Isa. 54.11-14)

The distinguishing mark of this city is that all its sons will be 'disciples of Yahweh', which is to say that in the new Jerusalem God's people's long history of disobedience and unfaithfulness will come to an end.

In Isa. 65.17-25 the portrayal of the revelation of God's glory in the new Jerusalem is mixed with motifs of paradise, so that the whole picture of the transformed and jubilant city is set within the framework of a new heaven and a new earth.

Whereas in the Book of Isaiah the temple plays no role in these images of the new Jerusalem,[110] Ezekiel places it at the centre of his promises as the token of the presence of God among his people, and 'the definitive sign of the reality of salvation'.[111] Ezekiel likewise looks for a gracious eschatological recreation of the people,[112] a final purification[113] through the bestowal of a new heart and the gift of the divine spirit.[114]

In the twenty-fifth year of the exile, Ezekiel underwent a
visionary experience in which he beheld the new Jerusalem and
its temple:

> . . . the hand of the Lord was upon me, and brought me in
> the visions of God into the land of Israel, and set me down
> upon a very high mountain, on which was a structure like a
> city opposite me. When he brought me there, behold, there
> was a man, whose appearance was like bronze, with a line of
> flax and a measuring reed in his hand; and he was standing in
> the gateway. (Ezek. 40.1-3)

Then with his measuring rod the prophet measured the
entire structure and determined its precise dimensions.

Just as in Isa. 65, there are linked with the vision of the holy
city in Ezekiel motifs related to paradise, which remind one of
Gen. 2.

> Then he brought me back to the door of the temple; and
> behold, water was issuing from below the threshold of the
> temple toward the east (for the temple faced east); and the
> water was flowing down from below the south end of the
> threshold of the temple, south of the altar. Then he brought
> me out by way of the north gate, and led me round on the
> outside to the outer gate, that faces toward the east; and the
> water was coming out on the south side . . . . As I went back
> I saw upon the bank of the river very many trees on the one
> side and on the other . . . . And on the banks on both sides of
> the river, there will grow all kinds of trees for food. Their
> leaves will not wither nor their fruit fail, but they will bear
> fresh fruit every month, because the water for them flows
> from the sanctuary. Their fruit will be for food, and their
> leaves for healing. (Ezek. 47.1-12)

In all these Old Testament prophecies of salvation which
have Jerusalem as their centre, we find common traits which
are not incidental or of secondary importance, but which are
essential features in the message of the prophet, and which had
an enduring effect on all later traditions. We shall briefly
summarize them.

1. In the glorified city, all the paths of God's people come
together at the end, and all the promises that God has given

them in the course of his history with them are fulfilled there. The new Jerusalem reveals that Israel is, and will remain, the chosen people, although she has many times in the course of her history been unfaithful to her calling, forsaken the living God, and has been condemned to frustration. Yet God's faithfulness has sustained her through all the judgments that have come upon her, and it will lead her finally to her original destination.

2. The goal, however, will be reached only through an eschatological act of God's grace and forgiveness. God will once again intervene in the history of the world in unconditional love, and will create for himself a pure people (cf. esp. Ezek. 36.22f.).

3. This renewal of the people will occur, however, not as a magic transformation, but through a repentance which has been bestowed upon them, as a result of which they are willing to accept God's grace.

4. The heart and centre of this hope is the covenant promise of the presence of God in the midst of his people, a promise which had been realized in Israel's history only in a hidden and provisionary manner through faith. 'I will be their God, and they will be my people' (Ezek. 37.27).[115] Salvation will consist of the fact of God's encounter with his people in unceasing mercy.

5. Nevertheless, God's redemptive will reaches out beyond the bounds of Israel. His people are to become the source of grace for all the nations.[116] There is, in this, no suggestion of a true missionary activity on the part of Israel, but rather that the nations will see Israel's glory as an invitation and a promise, and will be so attracted by it that they set out for the mountain of God to take part in her rejoicing.[117]

In the Judaism of the post-Old Testament period, too, Jerusalem remains at the centre of the hope of salvation. But the developing situation in which the Jews found themselves, religiously but above all politically, caused the Old Testament's eschatological conceptions to be shifted in various directions and forced a reshaping of the expectations attached to Jerusalem.

Quite divergent traditions developed, and not infrequently merged with one another, with the result that many questions regarding the concrete content of Jewish hopes can be answered only with difficulty. But there were essentially *four different ways* of looking at the Jerusalem of the future which stand out, and with which we must now deal briefly.

1. The *earthly city* of Jerusalem will stand one day, at the end of history, at the centre of the world in a glorified form — according to a number of various traditions, completely rebuilt.

Thus, for example, the description of the new Jerusalem in the Book of Tobit, which portrays its splendour after the pattern of Isa. 54.11ff., remains quite close to Old Testament thought:

> For Jerusalem shall be built with sapphires and emeralds,
>   her walls with precious stones,
>   and her towers and battlements with pure gold.
> The streets of Jerusalem will be paved with beryl and ruby
>   and stones of Ophir;
> All her lanes will cry 'Hallelujah!'
>   and will give praise,
>   saying, 'Blessed is God, who has exalted you forever.'
>   (Tobit 13.16ff.)

What is said in the Sibylline Oracles, Book 5, does not go beyond this. The Messiah

> made the city which God loved more radiant than the stars and the sun and the moon; he set it as the jewel of the world, and made a temple exceeding fair in its sanctuary, and fashioned it in size of many furlongs, with a giant tower touching the very clouds and seen of all. (Sib. 5.420-425)

The 'tower' is an expression for the temple, which is an integral part of Jewish hopes for the future.[118] Sibyllines 5.250ff. stresses the huge dimensions of the city. Its walls will reach to Joppa, and the city 'will reach up to the dark clouds'.

In the rabbinic literature, variegated and, in part, quite fantastic speculation with regard to the glory of the future Jerusalem is to be found. The city is built of indescribably precious materials, of jewels of every sort and of pearls. It will cover the entire land as far as Damascus and the sea, for all Israel will be gathered together in it. 'It is taught that Rabbi

Eliezer b. Jacob said, "Jerusalem will one day rise and ascend up to the throne of glory, and will say to God, 'The place is too narrow for me; make room for me to dwell in' " ' (Pesiq. 143a). Jerusalem will be the holy place of the presence of God to which all the peoples will flow.[119]

Expectation of this city was kept alive among the people through prayers for its erection. 'Take up thy dwelling soon in the midst of Jerusalem, thy city (as thou hast said), and build it speedily as an eternal building in our days. Blessed be thou, O Yahweh, who buildest Jerusalem' (b. Shmone-Esre, 14. Benediction).[120]

The seer of the Ethiopian Enoch (90.28f.) is allowed to behold the transfigured Jerusalem of the future:

> I stood up in order to watch, until he had folded up that old house. They carried away all the pillars, and all the beams and ornaments of the house were folded up with it. They carried it away and laid it in a place in the south of the land. I watched until the Lord of the sheep brought a *new house*, larger and taller than the first one, and set it up in the place where the first one, which had been folded up, had stood. All its pillars were new, and all its ornaments were new and larger than those of the first house, the old one which He had taken away; and the Lord of the sheep was in it.

The 'house' here denotes the entire city.[121] The old Jerusalem must vanish; then God will bring a new one in which he will take up his residence. This future house had already been envisioned by the prophet, but it was not conceived of as something already pre-existent in heaven, still less was anything said of its coming down from heaven at the end of time.

Several Qumran texts witness to this form of the expectations attached to Jerusalem. Owing to the multiformity of the statements one finds in these texts, one can of course proceed to a reconstruction of the eschatology of the Qumran community only with the greatest caution. We shall here attempt only to suggest the role of Jerusalem within the framework of eschatological hope. At the time when its books were written, the community stood in opposition to the temple-city which had, in this view, been profaned.[122] And yet these books witness to the fact that the community held tenaciously to the prerogatives of Jerusalem within salvation history. Thus it took up the promise of Deutero-Isaiah of a new Jerusalem (Isa. 54.11f.) and interpreted it allegorically in 4QpIs[d].[123] The foundations of sapphire are taken as referring to the founding of the community, the pinnacles of rubies to the twelve leading figures of the community whom Yadin identifies with the 'priests', and the gates of carbuncles to the 'heads of the tribes of Israel'.[124] One could understand this as a commentary on the Isaiah passage which interprets it as referring to the existing community, but one could just as well take it as pointing to a future situation in which, it was hoped, Jerusalem would be won back. The expression ראשי שבטי ישראל, in line 7 seems to suggest that the latter solution is the more probable, since there exist only two parallels to this expression in the texts, and both of these in writings that speak of the eschatological community of the future: in the War Scroll (1QM II.3),[125] and in the sketch of Israel's eschatological order in 1QSa 1.28. The fragment fits splendidly in this framework. The new Jerusalem of which Isa. 54 speaks, and which is the bearer of the promise, is the eschatological 'community' which represents the whole of Israel (cf. 1QSa 1.1).

Likewise, in a fragment of an interpretation of Isa. 10.28-11.14 (4Qp Isa. 1.7,11),[126] Jerusalem is seen in the hands of the holy community, fighting under the leadership of the promised kingly Messiah against the eschatological enemies.[127] The same situation is presupposed here as that encountered in 1QM.[128] According to the War Scroll, Jerusalem will be the capital city of the pure congregation and the headquarters of its armies fighting in the eschatological war, 'when the sons of light who are now in exile return from the wilderness of the nations to camp in the wilderness of Jerusalem' (1QM 1.3).[129] The warriors will ever and again return from the battle to the community in Jerusalem (1QM III.11; cf. VII.4).

In language that plays upon that of Isa. 60.5,10,14, as well as of other Old Testament passages, the Psalm in 1QM XII.13ff. celebrates this renewed Jerusalem:

O Zion, rejoice greatly!
Appear amid shouts of joy, O Jerusalem!
Exult, all you cities of Judah!

Open (14) [thy] gat[es] for ever
that the wealth of the nations may be brought to thee.
And let their kings serve thee
and let all they oppressors bow down before thee
and (15) [let them lick] the dust [of they feet]!
[O daughters] of my people, break out in cries of gladness!
Adorn yourselves with magnificent ornaments . . .

The Aramaic fragments published by M. Baillet are probably also to be understood in the light of this hope of a renewed Jerusalem.[130] These announce a new sanctuary with its cult, in dependence upon Ezek. 40ff.[131]

In accordance with the statements of the Old Testament, the Jewish sources unanimously affirm that the new Jerusalem will represent a people that is sanctified through and through. But this hope also embraces the nations, who will come as pilgrims to the holy mountain in the last days.[132] But, whereas the ancient synagogue had held fast to the universalistic hope of Old Testament prophecy, the shattering experiences of AD 70 and after led, at least in many circles, to a nationalistic narrowing of the hope of salvation.[133]

2. Whereas in all the passages we have discussed hope is directed towards an earthly Jerusalem, albeit one that is rebuilt, transformed, glorified, and even endowed with supraearthly traits, other texts speak of a heavenly reality.

The ancient synagogue knew of a 'Jerusalem that is above'. Yet the rabbis did not simply transfer their hopes to a city that is built in heaven, but rather continued at the same time steadfastly to hope for the restoration of the city on earth. Indeed, various passages state emphatically that God's Shekinah 'will not enter the heavenly city until the earthly city has been (re-)built'.[134] This heavenly city, therefore, cannot be the eschatological Jerusalem, the object of all hopes.

3. Nevertheless, it becomes the fulfilment of all hope in those texts that look forward to the coming down of the heavenly city to earth in the last day. It is difficult to say with assurance how old this concept is. It first appears in IV Ezra, and in the Revelation of John.[135] One may assume that John learned of it from Jewish tradition.

Since, for the Apocalypse of Ezra, salvation lies hidden

beyond this world and its history, nothing earthly can have part in the world of redemption: 'for there can be no human structure where the city of the Most High shall be revealed' (IV Ez. 10.54).[136] The new city, already beheld by the seer (IV Ez. 10. 25-27,40ff.), will be revealed along with the paradise, the 'hidden land' (IV Ez. 7.26; cf. 8.52). The Messiah will appear on the summit of Mount Zion; but Zion will appear (from heaven) and, completely restored, will be visible to all (IV Ez. 13.35f.). Salvation is thus already pre-existent in heaven with God, and will be revealed to the righteous in the new aeon.

4. The Apocalypse of Baruch, for which the heavenly world is the goal of all the ways of God, goes a step further beyond the Old Testament. The pre-existent and eternal home of all the godly is in heaven: 'This city, whose buildings now stand before you, is not the (future) one which is (even now) revealed with me and made ready here beforehand since the time when I made the decision to create paradise' (Syr. Bar. 4.3). Adam had already been allowed to see this city before his fall and so, later, had Abraham seen it on the night when he received God's covenant promise (Syr. Bar. 4.3-6; cf. also 6.9; 32.4).[137]

But now, having made this brief survey of the traditions of the Old Testament and of Judaism, let us turn to the subject of our particular concern, the city of God in the Book of Revelation.

B. THE MESSAGE OF REVELATION 21

(a) The Literary Problem

1

The question of the literary unity of Revelation 21.1-22.5 - which today is usually understood as a description of the consummation of God's Kingdom, or of the 'church of Jesus Christ which has been called together from among both Jews and Gentiles'[138] — is one that recent discussion has by no means settled. One might mention the odd reduplication of the picture of the new Jerusalem which we find in 21.1-8 and again in 21.9-27 (with a new introduction in 21.9). Moreover, in 22.1-5 we observe a peculiar repetition of elements from chapter 21 (cf. 21.3 with 22.3, and 21.23-25 with 22.5). And finally, the picture of paradise in 22.1ff. 'does not fit at all well with that of the heavenly city depicted as an enormous tower'.[139]

In addition, there is the fact that in 21.8,27 (and again in 22.15) John speaks of a 'within and a without', while 22.3 tells of the removal of everything accursed.

The two most important solutions to these difficulties in recent times can be studied in the commentaries of Charles and of Lohmeyer. Charles falls back on a rearrangement of the text that is radical and completely arbitrary,[140] while Lohmeyer seeks to explain 21.5-22.7 as a special type of vision which differs from all other visions and which he calls 'paraenetic'. It is one through which the seer seeks to give warning, comfort, and promise in and for his own time.[141] But neither of these solutions is satisfactory.

2

We shall begin our investigation with an analysis of the structure of the whole section of Revelation that is in question. And we start with the observation that the vision of the New Jerusalem itself is not introduced before 21.9f. Similar introductory formulae are to be found in 1.10; 4.2; and 17.3.

The last-mentioned passage, in ch.17, is especially revealing, for there is an exact parallelism both in form and in content between chs. 17 and 21. It is no accident that the introductory words in 21.9 ('Then came one of the seven angels who had the seven bowls full of the seven last plagues, and spoke to me, saying, "Come, I will show you the Bride, the wife of the Lamb" ') agree verbally with 17.1.[142] Both literary unities, 17.1-6 and 21.1-8, exhibit the same structure. Both contain a visionary description (17.2-6 and 21.9-27) which is introduced by words from the Old Testament or by reminiscences of Old Testament thoughts (17.1-2 and 21.1-8).

These introductory sentences are clearly distinguishable from the visionary descriptions by their lack of concreteness, which is no doubt occasioned by their stringing together of a series of Old Testament words designed to interpret the visions.[143]

But what in any event marks off the introduction to the Jerusalem vision from all others, even from that in chapter 17, is the fact that here the One Enthroned, God himself, begins to speak and, with promise and admonition, interprets the vision.[144] We shall have to say more about that later.

The visionary picture in 22.1-5 is formally quite distinct from the vision of the new Jerusalem. The articulation is accomplished on the one hand by the almost identically sounding words of admonition in 21.7 and 27, which conclude both the prologue to the Jerusalem vision and the visionary portrayal itself, and, on the other hand, by the new introductory formula in 22.1 ('and he showed me'), which also appears in 21.10. Thus the section 21.9-27 shows itself to be a closed unit which stands apart from the other one contained in 22.1-5.

In the visionary account of the new Jerusalem various groups of statements have to be distinguished.

First of all, in 21.10-14, the entire picture seen by John is sketched in a few short strokes: the city, the wall, the gates, the foundations.

Then, by the reintroduction of the angel (cf. v.9), vv.15-17, which tell of the shape and measurements of the city and its wall, are separated from the foregoing.

After this, there follows in 21.18-21 a description of the materials of which the city, together with its wall, its gates, its foundations, and its streets, is constructed.

Once again, the following verses (21.22-27) are grouped

together to form a special statement, which characterizes the city as the place of the eschatological encounter with God on the part of the inhabitants of Jerusalem, the nations, and 'the kings of the earth', who will stream through its gates into the holy city. The admonitory words of the last verse form the conclusion.

With 22.1, as we have seen, the seer begins the account of a new vision. But what he sees here is, of course, in its content closely related to the Jerusalem vision.

One might ask whether the collection of sayings which follows the account of this last vision does not provide a sort of epilogue to the entire Jerusalem vision of 21.9-22.5, which is intended — as is the prologue — as a word of promise and admonition to the church. We would then have to view 22.15 as the conclusion of the epilogue, for this verse ends — as does the prologue in 21.8, and the Jerusalem vision in 21.27 — with a repetition of the warning of the possibility of being 'excluded'. In this event, 22.16, the beginning of the conclusion of the entire book, would clearly refer back to its opening verses.

The close connection between the verses that follow 22.5 and what precedes receives further emphasis from the direct linkage of 22.6 to the vision of Paradise in 22.1-5. It is the same angel who introduced the visions (21.9f.) who now speaks; and the epilogue is marked by motifs from the Jerusalem-Paradise vision (cf. 22.6 and 21.5; 22.13 and 21.6; 22.14 and 21.25 and 22.2).

Our analysis has shown that the entire section that we are attempting to investigate exhibits a clear, formal articulation.

21.1-8   Prologue to the following visions
21.9-27   The vision of the new Jerusalem
22.1-5   The vision of Paradise
22.6-15   Perhaps an epilogue to the visions of the new world.[145]

(b) The Prologue

1

The solemn introduction to the Jerusalem vision in 21.1-8 through its very length, but especially through the mention of

God's voice, points to the fact that here the high point of the entire book, the fullness of all the secrets of God (cf. 10.7) has been reached.

It has already been emphasized that this introductory section is made up of quotations from, or allusions to, Old Testament passages. This is not suprising here, for throughout the book the seer never tires of referring to the Old Testament in order to show that his message is the fulfilment of its promises.

At the very opening of the vision (21.1f.) John takes up Isaiah 65.17:

> For behold, I create new heavens
>   and a new earth;
> and the former things shall not be remembered
>   or come to mind.

What is to come is clearly marked off from all that has gone before, and all that has been hitherto is superseded. The old world is judged and dissolved[146] (20.11-15) and the new creation shines forth. The 'sea', which in Revelation 20.13 was the manifestation of the world of the dead, and which according to 13.1 was the realm of the Antichrist,[147] is no more.

The new Jerusalem is a part of this new world or, to put it better, the holy city is its concrete form. Its nature is then indicated by means of concepts taken from the Old Testament.

But first, in contrast to all the promises of the Old Testament, the heavenly origin of the holy city is insisted upon (21.2). Like the Ezra Apocalypse, John separates the eschatological fulfilment of the Jerusalem promises from the earthly city.[148] The eschatological holy city is an entirely new creation.[149]

Yet the fact that the new world is linked with the name Jerusalem, so pregnant with meaning in salvation history, and is called by the biblical title of 'the holy city', is worthy of special consideration. Indeed, John himself draws our attention to certain specific relationships between the two cities. Thus, in 11.2, he calls the earthly Jerusalem 'the holy city' which, however, has profaned itself by its crucifixion of the Lord (11.8) and by its opposition to the two 'witnesses' (11.2). For this reason the nations will trample the city throughout the entire end-time, the forty-two months of Daniel.[150] And for this reason, too, the earthly Jerusalem no longer bears the title of God's holy city, but rather the shameful designation which links it with the godless city, the whore Babylon, 'the great city' (11.8; cf. 14.8; 16.19; 17.18), as well as the names of the godless and of the enemies of Israel in the Old Testament, 'Sodom and Egypt' (11.8).

It is only the *new* Jerusalem that rightly bears the title 'the holy city'. There is thus a radical break in the history of Israel, which throws its continuity utterly into question.

The picture, to be sure, is complicated by the fact that John connects the Jerusalem tradition not only with the future city, but also and at the same time with the church of the Lamb in the present age.[151] The church already stands on 'Mount Zion' (14.1), and as the community of the millennium is already the 'beloved city' (20.9). But neither expression speaks of the earthly city of Jerusalem, nor of any specific earthly place whatever, just as little as does the expression 'the camp of the saints' (20.9).[152]

John seems to distinguish the hope for Zion-Jerusalem that has already been fulfilled in history from the eschatological hope in such a way that he applies the name 'new Jerusalem' and 'the holy city' only to the city of the future, while connecting the Zion concept with the church of the Lamb, for not only the designation for the redeemed in 14.1, but also that of 'the beloved city' refers back to Old Testament passages having to do with Zion: 'Mount Zion which he loves' (Ps. 78.68), and 'the foundation on the holy mount' which 'the Lord loves' (Ps. 87.2).

In any event, John makes a *very clear distinction between the two entities*, for, as we have seen, 21.1 introduces an entirely new situation for the people of God. Whereas the community of Zion even in the millennial kingdom still lives on this old earth, the new Jerusalem belongs to the new heaven and the new earth. Indeed, the heavenly city descends to the new earth, so that from then on the separation of heaven and earth is for ever abolished.[153]

But however detailed the seer's description of the form of the new city, his real interest does not lie in places or things. His real concern is with *men*, the people of God, who will partici-

pate in the benefits of salvation.[154] Thus the 'city' is 'personified', as it often is in the Old Testament, and compared with a
'bride' who is 'adorned for her husband' (cf. esp. Isa. 52.1;
61.10). The holy Jerusalem points to the new situation which
God's people will occupy in the reality of the new creation.

We shall have to investigate how this entire concept is related
to its source, the Old Testament's hope of a coming new and
gracious turning of God to his people of Jerusalem, to whom,
according to his promise, he will betrothe himself once more,
and forever (Hos. 2.14-23).[155]

2

After this announcement of the vision that has been granted to
John, the reality of what has been seen is interpreted over and
over again by means of fresh words taken from the Old Testament.[156] Two groups of sayings, which are ascribed to two
different speakers, are clearly to be distinguished. The first
speaker is represented as 'a mighty voice from the throne'
(21.3f.), the second is God himself (21.5-7).

(*a*) In the *first series* of sayings the new Jerusalem is first of
all characterized, with an allusion to Lev. 26.11f., as the
fulfilment of the promises given to God's people as they
wandered in the wilderness: 'I will take up my abode among
you, and will not abhor you. I will walk alone in your midst,
and will be your God, and you shall be my people.'[157] The holy
city is the place of the divine encounter.

But the presence of God means the abolition of all troubles
and temptations which, through tears, death,[158] suffering, cry-
ing and pain, have darkened the life of the old world, the
πρώτη γῆ (21.1).[159] The Old Testament is again not quoted
literally, but there is clear reference to the eschatological
tradition of Isaiah 25.8; 35.10; 65.19.

(*b*) The *second group* of Old Testament sayings is introduced
directly as the word of the one who sits on the throne (21.5-8).
This is the only place in the entire book where God himself is
the speaker. It lends to the promises that follow, and to the
visions that they interpret, the force of an irresistible certainty.

It is not surprising that at this decisive turning point in the
divine history we should meet once again the number 7 as a
formative element. And, as in other places in Revelation, the

series of seven is arranged in sections of 3 + 4, as is indicated by the fact that the first three sayings are provided with introductory formulae (καὶ εἶπεν ὁ καθήμενος 5a, καὶ λέγει 5β, καὶ εἶπέν μοι 6) while the remainder are linked on directly, without formulae.

1. The first of God's words embraces and opens up the whole of the prophecy about the future of mankind after the destruction of the old world. Underlying it is an interpretation of Isa. 43.18f. The way in which John divides this Old Testament text, and the fact that he does so, seems significant. He links the first part of the verse with the first voice that speaks; but it is God alone who speaks of the new creation! It is possible that the seer is thinking especially of the way the same thought is worded in Isa. 65.16f.:

> . . . the former troubles are forgotten
> and they are hidden from my sight.

> For behold, I create new heavens and a new earth;
> Former things shall no more be remembered,

and that he relates the 'former troubles' of the Isaiah text to the suffering in 21.4.

2. In the second word, the church's assurance is grounded in God's own promise. God explicitly orders the seer to confirm in writing that these words are trustworthy. It is an essential feature of the theology of Revelation that these same statements also characterize the word of Jesus, who is 'the word of God' in person (1.5; 3.7,14; 19.13).[160] God himself has given his guarantee in his Christ.

3. The assertion that now follows γέγοναν[161] must, like all the statements in the prologue, be understood as a promise and an interpretation of the reality seen in the visions of Jerusalem. The plural form suggests that γέγοναν is to be related to the λόγοι which are mentioned immediately before, and which announce the new creation. Just as in 16.17 γέγονεν points to the fulfilment of the prophecies of the bowls, so here it points to the fulfilment of all the words of God in the Jerusalem visions.

4. The final guarantee of the truth of all of God's words lies in God's own nature. This is suggested by the application to

God of the Alpha-Omega formula, which characterizes him in his relationship to the world (cf. 1.8).[162] God stands at the beginning of the world ('for thou didst create all things, and by thy will they existed and were created', 4.11),[163] and he stands at its end. But, for John, the creator and perfecter of the world is not to be separated from its redeemer. For this reason the formula is also transferred to Christ. He is 'the First and the Last' (1.17), 'Alpha and Omega' (22.13),[164] 'the beginning of the creation of God' (3.14). The world's goal is therefore not judgment, the abyss, emptiness — in spite of its rebellion, which John in his book describes in such a sinister way — but a gracious new creation.[165] Because this is God's nature, and nothing other, the church may wait with complete assurance for the perfect fulfilment of his words.

5. With the last-mentioned word the transition to the fifth statement is made. The church needs the sure prophecy, for she still stands as the people of the promise, longing and thirsting for eternal life, and only he who endures the thirst, who cannot and will not seek refreshment from the waters of this world, will receive the promise.[166]

6. In the next saying the same thought is expressed through the figure of battle. The church is in conflict with hostile powers. But her Lord is already victorious over these powers (5.5). The church therefore has her part in his victory (12.10f.). But she has now to stand fast against the daily temptations, which could even lead to her death. The new world is promised as an inheritance only to the 'victor', and to him there is given the promise of divine sonship which originally concerned only the king (II Sam. 7.14), but which is here transferred to the kingly church.[167]

7. The last saying, which is linked with the prophecy and the interpretation of the new creation, seems rather surprising in that it takes the form of a stern warning. The promise of life stands over against the threat of a second death. The future of the godless is judgment, the 'lake of fire'.[168]

(c) The Vision Account

One of the angels of the seven last plagues summons John to ready himself for a new vision. The identification of the angel points back to the great antithesis of the city of God: Babylon, 'the great city that has dominion over the kings of the earth' (17.1-18). In ch.17 it is also one of the angels of the bowl-judgments who introduces the vision.

In the angel's summons the city is called 'the bride', just as in the prologue to the vision, but at the same time is also designated by the pictorial expression of 19.7 as 'the wife of the Lamb'.[169]

'Bride' and 'wife' both suggest the people of God in its relationship to Christ (19.7; 22.17).[170] Both express the thought that access to the holy city can be gained only through being joined to Jesus.

Carried by the Spirit to a high mountain, John now sees the city. Both the visionary experience and the account of it are determined through and through by Ezekiel 40.2ff. Ezekiel was also brought in a state of ecstasy to a high mountain before which the new Jerusalem was spread out. And Ezekiel likewise saw a man with a measuring rod. What a man measures, to be sure, is not the city, but the temple. But the dependence of Revelation 21 on Ezekiel 40 is clear.

The entire vision account of 21.9-27 can (without any forcing!) be divided into seven parts:

9f.   The removal of the seer to the mountain
10-14 The description of the holy city
15-17 The shape and measurements of the city
18-21 The materials of which it is built
22-23 The presence of God
24-26 The significance of the city for the nations
27   The word of warning.

Then follows a new vision account opening up a new dimension of the Jerusalem hope. We begin our investigation of these features with a discussion on the city.

(d) The City

1

The city that comes down from heaven is introduced in the very first words as the place where God's glory dwells. It is not a place that God's glory has first to enter (as in Ezek. 43.1ff.), but one to which it essentially belongs: ἔχουσαν τὴν δόξαν τοῦ θεοῦ (21.11).

The city's splendour is compared to a jasper, clear as crystal.[171] 'Jasper' very probably denotes a white, or transparent, stone. Along with the reddish carnelian — no doubt because its colour is that of the light, or of fire[172] — jasper serves also in Revelation 4.3 as an expression for the shining splendour of God! God is present in the new Jerusalem. There is therefore no more any need for the sun, or the moon, 'for the glory of God is its light, and its lamp is the Lamb' (21.23). The wording shows that John understands his vision as the fulfilment of Isa. 60.19:

> The sun shall no longer be your light by day,
> nor the moon shine on you when evening falls;
> the Lord shall be your everlasting light,
> your God shall be your glory.

It is to be expected that the temple would be thought of in this connection also, since it is, after all, the visible sign of the presence of God among his people. What the temple expressed as a promise for faith has arrived at final fulfilment in the heavenly city. For this reason John identifies God and the Lamb with the temple of the new Jerusalem.[173] The city has no further need of any other temple (21.22). This is something that sets the eschatology of John apart from all Jewish expectations.[174]

Now the fact ought not to be overlooked that two separate possibilities were open to the seer for the interpretation of the temple itself. And he has in fact used both. Thus he can, on the one hand, call *God* and the *Lamb* themselves the temple; but at the same time it was but a short step for him to relate not only the holy city, but especially the temple, to the *people of God* in whose midst God dwells. This second interpretation is in fact given in the words of promise to the partners in salvation of the new Jerusalem in Rev. 3.12, where the victor is promised that he will be made 'an everlasting pillar' in God's temple, and a bearer of the name of God and of the new Jerusalem.

It seems to me that the same concept also dominates the entire portrayal of the shape of the city. It is said of it only that it forms an enormous cube of twelve thousand stadia on each side, and that it is made — as are its streets — of 'pure gold, clear as glass' (21.18). The colours of jasper and of gold suggest the indescribable radiance of the whole city in the shining splendour of God's glory. But these statements lead us to still further, quite definite, contexts.

In order to explain the strange cubic form, scholars have ever and again referred to ancient conceptions of the shape of heaven, or to the quadratic layout of the city of Babylon and of the Babylonian temple towers.[175] But as attractive as ancient oriental notions of the cosmos are for the interpretation of Rev. 21, and as certainly as the idea of the firmament originally stands behind the whole concept of a heavenly city, it is still to be considered that the original astral significance of the picture had already retreated into the background in the later Jewish traditions, and that for John, who is so extraordinarily deeply rooted in the Old Testament and who understands his visions as the fulfilment of the promises of the Old Testament, another cubic form, known from the Old Testament, stands much closer to hand, namely, *the Holy of Holies* of the Solomonic temple, of which it is said that the king 'overlaid it with pure gold'.[176]

One can see how familiar the seer is with such traditions when one considers that, in his visions, he sees the heaven as a temple (7.15; 11.9; 13.6; 16.17), where God sits enthroned (4.1ff.; 4.15; cf. Isa. 6.1). In the heavenly temple there stand altars (6.9; 8.3ff.; 9.13) and the heavenly Ark of the covenant, which will be made visible at the end of history (11.9). It is characteristic of ancient oriental thought that the earth has its correspondent in heaven, that 'the prototypes of all countries, rivers, cities and temples exist in the skies in great constellations, while these earthly things are only copies of them'.[177] Thus the earthly temple is 'a copy and a shadow of heavenly things' (Heb. 8.5; cf. Exod. 25.40).

To be sure, equal emphasis must be laid upon the fact that John, by a radical change of the form of the image, distinguishes very clearly between the heaven which belongs to the old earth in the time prior to the new creation and the new heaven in the world of perfection. It is significant in this connection that, for John, the heavenly Jerusalem, which represents the 'new' heaven, is not a pre-existent entity, as in certain Jewish conceptions, and that in the new Jerusalem a temple is no longer set apart from the other parts of the city.[178] Rather, John places the whole city in a new relationship to the temple concept, in that he identifies it with the cubic, golden Holy of Holies, which is filled with God's glory.[179] Not only the high priest — and he not merely once in a year — enters this eschatological Holy of Holies, but the entire people dwells in it for ever.

2

It is therefore completely wrong to relate the number 12, which is constitutive for the measurements of the city and its wall, to mythical traditions of any sort.[180] The number 12, too, has its roots in the Old Testament. John expressly so interprets it in 21.12: it points back to the basic structure of Israel, the twelve tribes. It is reflected in the number of the gates, of the foundation stones, in the length of the sides of the city, and in the wall whose dimension is the square of 12 (21.12-17). That the whole description of the holy city is so strongly marked by Israel's number is revealing, for John loves to introduce numbers as means of expressing essential theological concepts.

Israel's number has already appeared in 7.1-8, where the seer beheld the sealing of twelve thousand 'servants of God' of 'each of the tribes of the sons of Israel' before the outbreak of the eschatological tribulations. The full number of the tribes is linked with the Jewish hope 'that in the end-time the lost tribes of the northern kingdom will be brought back and Israel completely restored' (Isa. 49.6; IV Esd. 13.39ff.; Apoc. Bar. 78.1ff.).[181]

It is, however, clear that John is here thinking of the church. This is already indicated by the general statement of 9.4, where preservation from the plagues of the angel of the underworld, which drive those concerned into such extreme despair that they 'long to die' (9.6), is promised only to those who bear

God's seal on their foreheads.[182]

But this cannot mean that every special eschatological expectation for the Jewish people is therewith completely and irrevocably annulled.[183] For John, hope for Israel is in no sense dissolved into the church, just as little as Paul excludes a special hope for Israel (cf. Rom. 9-11) when he calls the church 'the Israel of God' (Gal. 6.16),[184] or 'the temple of God' (I Cor. 3.16f.; II Cor. 6.16), or speaks of the church's belonging to the Jerusalem above (Gal. 4.26). Like Paul, John indeed stresses in ch.7 the linkage of the church to Israel and its hope in salvation history and, like Paul, he points to the continuity as well as to the discontinuity in salvation history.[185]

The number 12 dominates the vision of the new Jerusalem completely.[186] Because for John this number is quite obviously anchored in the Old Testament history of redemption, the problem that is thereby posed for interpretation must on no account be overlooked or glossed over.[187] Israel's number points the reader once again and inescapably to the still unanswered question of salvation history, namely, that of *the fate of Israel,* the chosen people. This is of fundamental significance for the understanding of the whole of chapter 21.

3

Only in the light of the Jewish problem do the secret relationships which are formed by the names of the new Jerusalem become understandable. The new Jerusalem is called 'the holy city' (21.2,10). As we have seen, the name refers back to the vision in chapter 11 which tells of the fate of the earthly Jerusalem-Israel in the end-time. The earthly Jerusalem-Israel was once called this (11.2).[188] But through its unbelief it lost its honour and its name. It seems to have been completely abandoned, written off. There is scarcely a sharper disparagement or condemnation of Jewish unbelief in the entire New Testament than here in the Revelation of John. And yet the whole dismal picture of Jewish disobedience is left open to the future in John's prophecy because of three fundamental limitations that are placed on the judgment.

First a remnant of Israel is spoken of, which is to be separated from the rejected portion of the people of the temple by measuring (11.1f.). The true worshippers will be preserved!

That the seer knew exactly what he was saying is clear from his characterization of the Jews in 2.9 and 3.9. He speaks of the Jews who have attacked the church of Jesus and its message as pseudo-Jews, who are not Jews but the synagogue of Satan. True Jews would have to be open to the revelation of the truth in the Lamb of God.[189] These are the true worshippers who will not 'be cast out'.[190]

The *second* limitation placed on the judgment upon Israel lies in the prediction that Jerusalem, even during the time of its profanation, will not be left without the proclamation of God's message (11.3ff.). To be sure, the bearer of the divine word is no longer the people of the temple as such and as a whole, but the church of Jesus Christ, which is represented by the two 'witnesses', and which embraces the remnant of Israel and the Gentiles.[191]

A *third* limitation of the judgment, finally, is brought by the temporal restriction of the profanation to forty-two months, which is to say, to the end-time which will be terminated by the parousia of Christ.[192] Until then, Jerusalem is no longer the holy city. Her privileges and duties are transferred to the church, upon which John, like Paul, is able to confer the predicates of honour of the people of God.[193] But this profanation is limited to the time of the Gentiles.

Thus the three limitations upon the judgment at least leave the door open for a hope for Israel's future. To be sure, in Revelation this hope is no longer directed towards the earthly realm, towards a purification and a glorification of the city in Palestine which has become unholy, but towards a new, creative intervention of God, towards the new *Jerusalem* that will once more bear the name of the holy city and restore it to honour.

These relationships must not be forgotten if we wish to do justice to the intention of the seer. The new Jerusalem, the cubic holy of holies which is perfectly shaped by Israel's number, cannot rightly be understood if one sees in it merely a general image of the consummation of the world. The eschatology of Revelation is more complex. The new Jerusalem points rather to a particular hope: the final fulfilment of the Old Testament's promises for Israel. John in his own way interprets the prophetic message that God will in the end glorify himself by showing his mercy and faithfulness to his chosen people through an eschatological act of grace.[194]

4

The sayings of 21.5-6 thus reveal themselves to be a very concrete prophecy. When God begins to make all things new, his first concern will once again be for the people of Israel. The Alpha-Omega and the Arche-Telos formulae can be fully understood only in this context. They assert not only that God will stand at the end just as at the beginning, but also that God will reveal himself at the end as the same God as at the beginning, that the end cannot be without this beginning, and that 'all' that has happened between Alpha and Omega will not be lost and forgotten, but will remain embraced by the God who has brought to completion in the death of the Lamb what he had begun in the history of Israel, namely, the overcoming of this whole rebellious reality through *redemption*. The vision of the new Jerusalem is an expression of God's faithfulness to the work which he has begun.

5

The message to the church in Philadelphia (3.7-13) also witnesses to exactly this same all-embracing hope for Israel. This church is attacked by Jews who, through their opposition to Jesus and his church, deprived themselves of the divine presence; they are engaged in the business of the 'world' and therefore have become a synagogue of Satan. But this is not God's final verdict upon them. In a quite extraordinary way Isaiah 60, which John uses especially in his delineation of the picture of Jerusalem, is interpreted to apply to them. Isaiah 60.14 declares:

> The sons of those who oppressed you
> > shall come bending low to you
> and all who despised you
> > shall bow down at your feet;
> they shall call you the City of the Lord,
> > the Zion of the Holy One of Israel.

In Rev. 3.9 this prophecy is applied to the church of Jesus, to which the members of the synagogue of Satan will one day come, in the recognition that the church is loved by God (Isa. 43.4). Here the place of Israel is taken by the church, and that of the enemies by the Jews. But the essential thing is that still unbelieving Jews will in the end-time bow and recognize Jesus as Lord. This 'abrupt reversal of the Jewish eschatological hope' does not refer to the success of missionary activity among the Jews, but is a clear 'promise of an eschatological glorification'.[195] That the promises precisely of the church's message should issue in the new Jerusalem (3.12) is highly significant,[196] for the vision of the holy city is obviously the unfolding of this hope.

Certainly, for the authority of Revelation the entire community of Jesus Christ belongs first of all to the new Jerusalem. She is in fact the bride, the wife of the Lamb; she has thirsted after the water of life, to which Jesus leads those who are his own.[197] But the shape and the name of the city, and the numbers used to describe its dimension, spring from this framework, which is not adequate to contain the breadth of the promises to Israel.

(e) The Wall

1

In view of the length of the Jerusalem vision as a whole, the great detail with which the city wall and its significance is discussed in Rev. 21 is surprising. This is all the more the case, since the vision of promise which the seer has before his eyes (Ezek. 40-48) does not specifically mention the wall at all, and speaks of the city gates only in the last verses (Ezek. 48.30-34).[198] John's interest in this wall, its measurements, its materials, and its functions within the framework of the vision as a whole, demands explanation. Obviously it is not enough to understand the wall in a general sense as a necessary and indispensable feature of an ancient city, since the wall in no sense serves the purpose of an ancient city wall, namely, a defence against enemies, for its gates remain open continually.[199]

But undoubtedly the wall defines a boundary, between what is inside and what is without. We stand here before one of the

most remarkable features of the entire vision, and one that has
been interpreted in various ways, in spite of the fact that John
has expressed himself with unmistakable clarity. Perhaps this is
because of our unwillingness to accept ideas that are so foreign
to our way of thinking.

The strange thing about this idea is that John reckons with
the possibility of existence outside the boundaries of the walls
of the new Jerusalem. This is witnessed to by the three words of
warning in 22.15 ('outside are the dogs. . .'); 21.27 ('nothing
unclean shall enter it. . .'); and 21.8 ('But as for the cowardly,
. . . their lot shall be in the lake that burns with fire and
brimstone. . .'). This latter passage, moreover, makes clear how
John conceives of the 'outside': an existence in the lake of fire.
The seer speaks of this also in 20.10; 20.14; 19.20.

This side-by-side existence of the holy city and a place
beyond its walls is an essential feature of the prophecy of the
new Jerusalem. We have, therefore, first of all to inquire after
the reasons for this strange idea and to determine its significance within the framework of the eschatological concepts of
John. This will provide us with an idea of how the seer conceives of the last events.[200]

2

Above all, it must be kept in mind that the 'lake of fire' is
clearly distinguished from the abyss. According to Rev. 9.1-12,
the abyss is the home of the demonic powers, who are under
the leadership of their king, Abaddon-Apollyon.[201] It is therefore also the home of the beast that ascends from the pit at the
end-time and kills the two witnesses in Jerusalem (11.7).

The 'underworld' is manifested in the sea from which,
according to 13.11, the beast appears, and which at the same
time represents the world of the dead (20.13). This is why it
will no longer exist in the realm of the new creation (21.1).[202]
These passages show that the seer has apparently identified the
realm of the unsaved dead with the kingdom of the demons.

According to 20.1-3, the dragon will be imprisoned in this,
his very own kingdom, with the result that all power on earth
will be taken from him. After his release he will be thrown into
the lake of fire together with his hellish host, as will the
Antichrist-Beast, his false prophet, Death and Hades, and all

'who are not found written in the book of life'.[203]

In contrast to the abyss, which is the home of the diabolical powers and the provisional place of judgment of the unsaved dead until the parousia of Christ,[204] the 'lake of fire' is the place where God's eschatological judgment will be executed upon all the lost.

As the image indicates, John understands the fate of those who have been condemned to the lake of fire as one of unspeakable pain, in contrast to that of those who have been redeemed from all the misery of fallen existence in the new Jerusalem, where they experience no more tears, or death, or pain, or weeping, or tribulation (21.4). Separation from God in the lake of fire means suffering 'day and night, εἰς τοὺς αἰῶνας τῶν αἰώνων,[205] that is to say, without ceasing and for an inconceivably long time.[206] The aeon formula, which appears in various contexts, is to be interpreted in the light of the context in which it occurs. In itself, it does not denote time without end, but an indescribably long duration.[207] At any rate, the image of an aeonic lake of fire does not signify a final annihilation or a dissolution into nothingness.[208]

3

This eschatological place of judgment is equated in four passages in Revelation with a concept probably already known in pre-Christian Judaism, that of the δεύτερος θάνατος. Since in all four passages the execution of the divine judgment is thought of, rather than the personal aspect of a second 'Thanatos' (which predominates in the formula 'Thanatos and Hades' throughout the book), the expression is correctly translated as 'the second death, experience of death'. By means of the number it is brought into connection with a first dying. This first death can only refer to that event which is placed over against the second death in 2.10f. 'Be faithful unto death, and I will give you the crown of life. He who conquers shall not be harmed by the second death.'[209]

What both kinds of death have in common is not only the cessation of life but also their character as *judgment*. Even the first death is a sign of the divine curse. That is clearly expressed in the threat found in 2.22f. but above all by the fact that Death personified is accompanied by his servant, the ruler of

the underworld, Hades.[210] Together they define the character
of the first death as one of judgment.

Now, to be sure, we have to bear in mind that the situation of
believers has already been changed. They too must die, as all
men do, but in their faith the unheard-of has taken place; the
judgment has already been overcome, for Christ has 'ransomed'
them from it through his own death (5.9f.; 1.18). He has the
key of Death and Hades in his hand (1.18), and therefore has
power over the fate of death.[211] The redeemed, therefore, are
freed from the power of Hades; for them, dying can only mean
entry into life, into heaven.[212] They are completely freed from
the second death.

The observation that the lake of fire is spoken of as the
'second death' only when godless *men* — not demonic powers —
are in question has prompted W. Michaelis to ask whether 'the
lake of fire represents the second death for the godless, and
only for them'.[213] He also points out that all the spirit-powers,
who are likewise delivered over to the lake of fire, did not
experience any first death, so that 'the expression, "second
death", must in their case mean something other than in the
case of the godless (20.15), who have already died once.'

This is possible. Nevertheless, it is worth considering that the
lake of fire signifies for both the same judgment, which is
independent of the first death. The closest analogy to the
concept of two judgments is their counter-image which annuls
them, namely, the first and the second resurrection. The seer
speaks only of the first resurrection, but the number points to a
second. One can have part in the second resurrection only if
one did not experience the first. The numbers mark a temporal
sequence of events.[214]

<h1 style="text-align:center">4</h1>

Difficult to understand though the whole idea may be for us at
first glance, it is nevertheless quite clear that for John this
eschatological place of condemnation does not disappear with
the abolition of the old world. On the contrary, the lake of fire
is one of those eschatological realities which first appear with
the parousia of Christ, but which are not a part of the new
heaven and the new earth, the world of the redeemed.

It is therefore not surprising that in 21.5-8, 9-27 there should be announced not only the new world of eternal life, but also and at the same time the possibility of eschatological judgment. Transpositions of the text or separation of sources are completely arbitrary and unnecessary. Only in the light of this overall view is it explainable why the existence and the nature of the city wall is given such significance in the description of the new Jerusalem, and why there is talk of an entry and of a being excluded.[215] The juxtaposition of the holy city and the place of condemnation which is 'without' is an essential part of the prophecy of the new Jerusalem. In his vision John gives an entirely new interpretation of the eschatological 'pilgrimage of the nations' of the prophets.[216]

The wall is thus set as a sign of separation. But it is to be noted in what way it fulfils this function. This is indicated in the description of its nature. It is built of jasper stones.[217] We have already seen that, for John, jasper is not merely one precious stone among others, but is an expression for the glory of God (4.3; 21.11). Thus, for the seer, the wall of jasper does not serve as a menacing defence against enemies, but rather as an announcement to the world of condemnation outside the city of the radiant glory of God's community in the new Jerusalem. Its message is not one of rejection and death, but one which, with its glowing promise, awakens longing for the miracle of the encounter with God.

The various other individual traits in the vision of the wall likewise serve this same function. The seer cannot say enough in his description of its sparkling beauty. It has long been recognized that the whole description of the individual traits goes far beyond the Old Testament and Jewish prototypes. But we must, nevertheless, recognize their function within the whole in order to understand their significance.

(f) The Twelve Foundation Stones

1

The wall, divided by the twelve gates, which encloses the city, has twelve stones as its foundation.[218] This reinterpretation of Isa. 54.11 both in the use of the number of Israel, as well as in the statements regarding the various kinds of precious stones which make up the foundation, is without parallel in Jewish tradition.

Once again the number 12, like the 12 x 12 cubits of the height of the wall, is a reference to the peculiar significance of the city as the fulfilment of prophecy to Israel.

The enumeration and the sequential arrangement of the precious stones is more difficult to understand. Most scholars refer to the description of the golden breastplate of the high priest in Exod. 28.17-21 and 39.10-13: 'And you shall set in it four rows of stones . . ., the first row, sardin, chrysolite and green felspar; the second row, purple garnet, lapis lazuli and jade; the third row, turquoise, agate and jasper; the fourth row, topaz, carnelian and green jasper, all set in gold rosettes. The stones shall correspond to the twelve sons of Israel, name by name; each stone shall bear the name of one of the twelve tribes engraved as on a seal.' The old assumption that the seer is thinking of this high-priestly garment[219] does not seem to me inappropriate, since in the vision of the holy city other cultic imagery is made use of and the entire city is viewed as an enormous Holy of Holies in which God and the Lamb are present.

The variation in the enumeration of the names of the precious stones is not decisive, in view of the uncertainty that surrounds the ancient mineralogical terminology. The sequential arrangement, which up until now has received no convincing explanation, is of more central importance. Whether John has taken over the arrangement from astral-mythological tradition remains most uncertain.[220] If the seer was actually thinking of the high-priestly garment, the pre-eminent position of the jasper (in contrast to Exod. 28 and 39) would be explained, for, according to Rev. 7.5, John begins the series of the tribes of Israel with Judah because Christ stems from Judah (5.5); that he should connect Judah with the jasper, the stone of the divine glory, is easy to understand.

If John was here thinking of Exod. 28, he has apparently ascribed to the city a priestly function on behalf of the people of the twelve tribes. It points them the way to God.[221] That would fit very well with the interpretation of the city wall presented above.

2

But it is of especial significance that the foundation stones do not bear the names of the twelve tribes, but those of the 'twelve apostles of the Lamb' (21.14). The circle of the Twelve whom, according to the Gospel accounts, Jesus chose as the represent-ation of the eschatological people of salvation,[222] are also brought into a significant relationship to the twelve tribes of Israel within salvation history in Matt. 19.28. John thus does not stand alone in ascribing to the apostles an eschatological function with relation to Israel. He makes it clear through his pictorial message that the foundations of the wall which separ-ates the world 'without' from the community of God, but which at the same time beckons to the realm of the unsaved with the splendour of the divine glory, point to the ambas-sadors of Christ, the bearers of the message of redemption through the Lamb.[223] In this pictorial element the same basic theological conviction finds expression, as was hinted at in the word about the Lamb's book of life; only those who belong to the Lamb, who have found redemption through the message of the crucified one, have part in the community of God.

(g) The Twelve Gates

1

Another trait is added which enlarges the whole picture, namely, the description of the twelve gates. According to the prototypes of Isa. 62.6 the gates are guarded by angels,[224] and according to Ezek. 48.31-35 they are designated by the names of 'the twelve tribes of the sons of Israel'. The fact that each of them consists of enormous pearls adds to the glory of the city.[225]

In his interpretation of the gates, however, the seer refers above all to the entire Isaianic picture of the pilgrimage of the nations (60.11). The gates are never shut.[226] They are ready to receive the continuous flow from 'without' (21.24-26).

In John's interpretation of the prophetic message by means of the Jerusalem vision the motif of *the open gates* is given a quite new, and positively decisive significance for his entire hope for the future. We have seen that for him the world outside the walls of Jerusalem is the lake of fire (the second death), the eschatological place of condemnation. Thus John announces nothing less than that even for this world of the lost the doors remain open!

In these verses we learn how John concretely conceives of the restitution of the people Israel, to which the entire vision bears witness. First of all, all unbelieving Jews, the 'synagogue of Satan', belong to the lake of fire. It is therefore of a significance that cannot be overrated that the seer, in his portrayal of the gates, should reach back to Ezek. 48.31-35 and see them as adorned with the names of the twelve tribes of Israel. They are in an especial sense *their* gates and, in the fact that they are continually open, an *invitation to the people Israel to enter into salvation,* into the open arms of the Father, first and above all for his first-born son who has denied his own destiny and identified himself with the nations, but who has not been given up by his Father's love.

John testifies to a great hope for the return of Israel into its *own* city, into its *own* gates.[227] It will in the end once again be the people of the twelve tribes, created anew and redeemed. With that, the prophetic promises of the final return of the people of God are taken up and exceeded. Just as the remnant of Israel formed the basis of the church (7.1-8), so the renewed Israel will be the foundation of the new world.

This hope is based on the christology of the Apocalypse. John interprets the victorious Christ as the eschatological king of the redeemed people of Israel. He is 'the Lion of the tribe of Judah' and 'the Shoot of David' (5.5).[228] The interpreter who senses behind these titles a Jewish nationalism has noted something essential which must not be forgotten.[229] Christ *is* first and above all the fulfilment of all the promises to Israel! He cannot be separated from the Old Testament's history of revelation. He is the king from the tribe of Judah whom, according to the promise of Gen. 49.9f., 'the nations will obey', and he is the promised offspring of David to whom, according to Isa. 11.1,10, 'all the nations will rally' and who 'shall stand as an ensign to the peoples'. His origins in salvation history in no way stand in tension with his universal significance.

2

John does not stand alone in his expectation. Wherever in the New Testament the destiny of the Jewish people is thought of in the light of the new revelation of Christ, the same hope breaks through. A promise of Jesus himself has been handed down that points to a new redemptive encounter with him at the end of time: 'You will from now on see me no more until you say, "Blessed be he who comes in the name of the Lord" ' (Matt. 23.39; cf. Luke 13.35).[230]

But above all, it is Paul who never doubts the faithfulness of God to the promises that he has given, and recognizes in the redemptive deed of Christ the saving hope of Israel.[231] He speaks as an apocalypticist of the 'mystery' of Israel, in the certainty 'that the rebellion of the Jewish people against Christ is not the end of their history'.[232] 'For I do not want to leave you in ignorance concerning this mystery, lest you become complacent in your own conceit: a stultification has come upon a part of Israel until the full number of the Gentiles has come in; and so *all Israel* will be saved . . .' (Rom. 11.25f.). The movement of the entire discussion completely excludes any identification of 'all Israel' with the church, which is the new Israel;[233] Paul speaks here of the redemption of the entire people Israel, even — and especially — those who before this eschatological event were among those whose hearts were hardened.

It is, of course, very difficult to determine where Paul sees the place of the restitution of Israel within the course of the eschatological events and, above all, whether it is to be before or after the parousia of Christ. Romans 11.25 hints only that the stultification will come to an end when the full number of the Gentiles have come in. Is this the time of the parousia?

In I Cor. 15.23f. Paul seems to make a distinction between the parousia, which is accompanied by the resurrection of all believers, and an event which follows upon it, which brings the work of Christ to an 'end'. This telos-event apparently consists in 'Christ's delivering the kingdom to God the Father'.[234] But, before that, all hostile powers are to be overcome and 'subordinated' to God, that is, they will be stripped of their pretended autonomous power.[235] Paul speaks here only of demonic powers. But that does not exclude the assumption that he sees within this context the subjugation, and therewith the redemption, of human enemies also (ἐχθροί: the word is used of Israel in Rom. 11.28) — although this theme is left out of consideration in I Cor. 15.

When the apostle in Rom. 11.15 calls the acceptance of Israel ζωὴ ἐκ νεκρῶν, he certainly gives no chronological information with regard to their place in the plan of salvation, but rather thereby characterizes Israel's redemption as an eschatological resurrection event.[236] In my opinion, a comparison with Rom. 6.22f. brings us a step further: here death is viewed as the wages of sin, that is, as judgment, and the gracious gift of God, ζωὴ αἰώνιος, as the goal of those who have been freed from sin. For Paul, death is a judgment which can only be overcome by the eternal life which is bestowed through the resurrection (cf. I Cor. 15.49-58). Thus when he promises for 'all of Israel' this transformation from existence in death to existence in life, he accordingly hopes that Israel will arrive at the goal when this new creation begins, namely, after the parousia of Christ and the resurrection of believers. We may suppose, therefore, that in the Pauline eschatology the redemption of 'all Israel' is one of those events that lie between the parousia and the completion of the plan of salvation.

The question naturally raises itself with regard to John as well as Paul: Who belongs to 'all Israel', the totality of all Jewish individuals, or only a specific part?[237] As regards Rom. 11, it is certainly to be considered that 'all Israel' cannot be understood as a contrast to the *pleroma* of the Gentiles, but rather in the light of 'what now happens (in Israel) and is indicated by the words ἀπὸ μέρους',[238] namely, a hardening of a *part* of the people.[239] Thus, at least for Paul, no individual in the whole history of the Jewish people can be excluded in advance. But the problem hangs ultimately on a single question: who in the end will be recognized by *God* as a Jew, as a believer or as an unbeliever? The answer to this question in the eschatology of John as well as that of Paul cannot be our concern, for to both God alone is the one who judges and the one who acts in the eschatological events.

3

Through the entry of all Israel, the new Jerusalem, which embraces first of all the church made up of Jews and Gentiles ('the bride of the Lamb'), will become the fulfilment of all the promises to God's own people. But Revelation exceeds even this expectation and speaks of a *promise for all nations*.

In doing this, John takes up Old Testament hopes and interprets them in the light of the revelation of Christ. As we have seen in the first part of our study, the nations already play a great role in the eschatological promises of the Old Testament. God makes his servant 'a light to the nations' (Isa. 49.6). He will show himself to be the king of all the world, so that even the archenemies of Israel will become his people. Thus Isa. 19.18-25 sees a time coming when 'five cities in the land of Egypt will speak the language of Canaan and will swear allegiance to Yahweh of Hosts', for 'there will be an altar to Yahweh in the midst of the land of Egypt' and the Egyptians will turn to God in repentance, and 'Israel will be the third with Egypt and Assyria, a blessing in the midst of the earth, whom Yahweh of Hosts has blessed, saying, "Blessed be Egypt my people, and Assyria the work of my hands, and Israel my heritage" '. But the essential point is that 'in all the passages of the Old Testament, without exception, in which reference is made to the eschatological pilgrimage of the Gentiles, the goal of the pilgrimage is the scene of God's revelation of himself, Zion, the holy Mountain of God'.[240] Jerusalem-Israel, the chosen representative of the nations, remains even in the end-time the place of revelation.

For John, 'the place' of the eschatological revelation to the nations is the *new Jerusalem*. Borrowing from Isa. 60.3,5, he tells of the entry of the nations through Jerusalem's gates, so that they 'walk in its light' (21.14).

Indeed, the seer's hope even embraces 'the kings of the earth'. Throughout the book they are a clearly defined entity, a collective expression for the holders of world-wide political power who place themselves at the disposal of the Antichrist (17.2,18). In the end they will hurl their entire massed power against God and his church (16.14; 19.9); but then, under the effect of Christ's word, they will collapse and die together with their armies (19.19-21). Having been destroyed, they belong now to the 'dead', of whom 20.15 speaks. According to God's judgment they will fall prey to the 'second death'.

When, in ch.21, John speaks of their entry into the gates of the holy city, he is actually hoping for the redemption of the foes of Christ *par excellence*[241] ,for entry into Jerusalem means nothing less than being freed from the judgment of the lake of fire, the second death, and admission into God's world of the new creation.

The notion of *two* resurrections fits into this concept without difficulty. In 20.6 John calls the resurrection of the church of Jesus 'the first resurrection', and he praises all who will have part in it, for whoever is not caught up in it must await the awful reality of judgment in the lake of fire, and can achieve life only through the judgment. This redemption event which finally abolishes the reality of judgment must be a *second resurrection* which is presupposed by the mention of a first. For the second resurrection — in analogy to the first and second death, both of which signify judgment — can only be a saving reality.

4

But the source of all these hopes is in the final analysis not the words of the Old Testament prophets, but *Christ*. 'The incorporation of the Gentiles in the Kingdom of God ... was expected and announced by Jesus as God's *eschatological act of power, as the great final manifestation of God's free grace*'.[242] And, for John, Christ has long since won total victory over all his foes (5.5),[243] and has become 'the ruler of the kings of the earth' (1.5). But his victory is the victory of the one 'who loves us', the victory of the Lamb who has offered himself as a sacrifice and 'has redeemed us from our sins through his own blood' (1.5)! Revelation knows of no other victory!

So it is that not only redemption within history, but also the eschatological liberation from the lake of fire, remains completely and solely bound to the Lamb, who is the temple and the light of the holy city. Only those who are written in the Lamb's book of life will enter the world of perfection (21.27!). Revelation knows of no purgatory in which the sufferings of the damned have the effect of erasing sins, nor any other means by which the creature can accomplish his own liberation. The water of life is to be received δωρεάν as unconditional grace through Jesus Christ the crucified one (21.6). But the victory of grace will in the end be stronger than all the resistance of the unbelief of Israel, and of the nations and kings of the earth!

C. THE MESSAGE OF REVELATION 22

(a) Paradise

1

This victory of grace is the subject of the last vision of the entire book, in 22.1-5. Lohmeyer has correctly called attention to the fact 'that this section is marked off as an independent vision alongside the preceding ones' by means of the introductory formula καὶ ἔδειξέν μοι.[224] But the imagery is also new as over against ch.21. Features from the pictures of paradise in the Old Testament are introduced, such as the river of paradise from Gen. 2.10, which is interpreted as the water of life.[245] According to Ezek. 47.1ff., this flows from the temple, the dwelling place of God; according to Rev. 22.1, from the throne of God and the Lamb.[246] Like the heavenly sea in 4.6, the river shines like crystal. It symbolizes the fullness of the life-powers which flow through paradise.[247]

Trees of paradise, which in Ezek. 47.2,12 likewise are a part of the picture of the renewed land, are mentioned, too.[248] The trees of life evidently form an avenue along the great street and the river. The exact form of the visionary picture cannot be ascertained from the Johannine report.[249] The trees bear fruit every month so that an abundance of the powers of life are available, life that shall never end. The leaves of the trees, according to Ezek. 47.12, serve 'for the healing of the nations'.

What lifts the final vision above all those that have preceded it is its *universalism* of *salvation*. While in the vision of the new Jerusalem with its open gates the *promise* and the availability of unconditional grace is made manifest, the concluding vision prophesies the *realization* of this grace. Life and healing are now in fact imparted to all the nations. Jerusalem broadens itself out to become paradise. There is now no longer a 'within and without', for the end of every curse and condemnation is announced: καὶ πᾶν κατάθεμα οὐκ ἔσται ἔτι (22.3).

This decisive, positively universal word of prophecy, which opens up the deepest meaning of the final vision, points towards a future which exceeds and brings to perfection the events of

21.10-27. The lake of fire, or the second death, is now done away with, for Israel, the nations, and the kings of the earth have entered into the fullness of the light of the divine glory. Revelation exhibits a hope which embraces the entire creation.

The finality of the promise may even contain an indication of the destiny of the superhuman powers. To be sure, John does not express himself explicitly concerning the future of these powers, for his interest is concentrated exclusively upon people when he speaks of the coming salvation. Nevertheless, we find in his book no word about a final annihilation of these powers, but only the hope for the removal of every curse and the creation anew *of all things* (21.5). That can really only mean that the seer thinks of the transformation of these powers also, for they, too, are a part of created reality.[250]

2

That this interpretation does not do violence to the text is shown by two further universal prophecies in the book.

In a passage that is decisive for the entire christology of Revelation, the commissioning scene in ch.5[251] where the absolute victory of the Lamb is proclaimed, it is not only the choirs of the twenty-four elders and the four beings with the innumerable multitudes of angels that respond with praise, but — already anticipating the end — 'every creature that is in heaven, and on the earth, and under the earth, and on the sea, and all that lives therein' (5.13).

The unconditional nature of this statement is underscored by the complete four-part cosmos formula, to which the four-fold doxology corresponds ($\varepsilon\dot{v}\lambda o\gamma\dot{\iota}a$, $\tau\iota\mu\dot{\eta}$, $\delta\dot{o}\xi a$, $\kappa\rho\dot{a}\tau o\varsigma$).[252] Whereas the two acclamations of ch.4, which portray God, the Lord of history, are completely determined by the divine number 3,[253] in the image of ch.5 the motifs of 7 and 4 are woven in.[254] The domination of the cosmic four-beat, and its connection with the number 7, which is related to redemption (Christ, church, Spirit), is highly significant for the understanding of the conquering Lamb. The victory of the redeemer is therewith proclaimed as a world-embracing work and in 5.13 is proleptically praised by the whole creation.

The second prophecy, too, which embraces the entire world of the nations, is uttered in the form of a hymn. Directly before

the outpouring of the last plagues, through which the wrath of
God is brought to its completion, in the hour of deepest misery,
of the total outbreak of godlessness, John already hears the
victors over the Antichrist at the crystal sea jubilantly proc-
laiming the end of the ways and the works of God, 'the king of
the nations', in the words of Ps. 86.9:

> All the nations thou hast made shall come
>   and bow down before thee, O Lord,
>   and shall glorify thy name.

And they sing the song of Moses, the servant of God, and the
song of the Lamb, saying:

> Great and wonderful are thy deeds,
> O Lord God the Almighty!
> Just and true are thy ways,
> O King of the ages (or: nations).
>
> Who shall not fear and glorify thy name, O Lord?
> For thou alone art holy,
> All nations shall come and worship thee,
> For thy judgments have been revealed. (15.3,4)

The mighty finale of the paradise vision shows that the seer
has not only taken over these promises as cherished poetic
traditions, but that he believes quite literally in their fulfilment. In the light of this, too, we gain a full understanding of
his transcending the quotation from Isa. 43.19 through the
significant insertion of πάντα in 21.5: 'Behold I make *all things*
new.'[255] '*All* things' is not to be found in Isaiah.

With that, the problem of the oft-observed 'repetitions' in
the paradise image of elements from the Jerusalem vision is
likewise solved.[256] Now the promise which had previously been
limited by 21.8,27 is valid without limitation for *all*! The
throne of God, which is also the throne of the Lamb as a sign of
his victory (3.21), reveals the presence of the ruler of all (21.3b,
22), to whom now *all* creatures yield obedience as his servants
(21.22-24 and 22.1-3). To *all* of them it is given to see God in
fulfilment of Ps. 17.15 (cf. Ps. 41.13; I John 3.2), and *all* will
now bear his name (22.4, as 3.12),[257] and God will be a light to
all (22.5, as 21.23). The glory from which the nations were

excluded now embraces *all*.

A final paradise motif then concludes the whole account: '. . . and they shall reign for ever and ever' (22.5; cf. Gen. 1.26; Dan. 7.18,27). It is significant that the priestly aspect in this description (cf. 1.6; 5.10; 20.6) is not mentioned here, because priesthood is no longer needed in a world where God enlightens every creature.[258]

3

The all-embracing promise for the entire world in no sense minimizes the severity of the coming *judgment*, which is expected both in the Old Testament and the New. But, for John, neither in its historical nor in its eschatological form is the judgment God's last word, but rather serves in the final analysis as the agent of his grace.

It is for this reason that *repentance* is said to be the purpose of the eschatological plagues in 9.20 and 16.11. And for this reason God's *justice* in his judgment, which in 16.6f. is praised after the manner of an Old Testament judgment doxology (with reference to Ps. 119.137),[259] in 15.3f. is linked to the final saving goal of all divine judgments. The ways and the deeds of God will finally lead the nations to God, to the worship of the holy King of the nations!

Köhler has pointed out that in the Old Testament, too, judgment is salvation, because salvation is always linked with God. 'Judgment is the re-establishment of God's honour and holiness.'[260] One can transfer this to the Revelation of John as well, but only if one considers that, for the apocalypticist, *God's honour* is the *honour of the Lamb* (Rev. 5.9,10,12,13b), the honour of the one who offered himself up for the world in order to lead the lost back into the realm of light. In this sense one can probably apply the word in 3.19, which is taken from Job 5.17 or from Prov. 3.12, to the end of history: 'Those whom I love I reprove and chasten; so be zealous and repent.' *The aim of all judgment is repentance.*

(b) Epilogue

1

The direct connection between the last visionary picture and the words that follow (22.6.15) seems to indicate that the seer understood these last as an epilogue to the visions of the future. The word of warning in 22.15, which in similar form concludes the prologue of the vision of perfection (21.8), and also the Jerusalem vision (21.27), must probably then be understood as the concluding word of the epilogue. Upon it there follow some final sayings which conclude the entire Book of Revelation.[261]

Most interpreters divide the words of 22.6-15 between Jesus and the seer. According to this view vv.6 and 7 are spoken by Jesus, vv.8 and 9 by John, and vv.8-15 again by Jesus. One cannot be certain. But this interpretation raises an insoluble difficulty in the abrupt beginning of the words of Jesus in 22.6 (it is an angel that has been speaking immediately before), and also in the insertion of the experience with the angel (22.8f.) which, in these circumstances, is completely without motivation.

One would really expect that the speaker who is introduced by the words καὶ εἶπέν μοι is the angel of the vision of 21.9f. and 22.1. And v.6 can without any difficulty be understood as the word of an angel. The angel designates the message he has just brought as 'trustworthy and true', since he is 'the angel of God' (cf. 1.1) whom 'the God of the spirits of the prophets' himself has sent.

Only under this interpretation does the word of John in 22.8f. become meaningful in its context, since it refers to his encounter with the angel who has just been mentioned.

After the angel's word there comes a double saying of Jesus (22.7), which is in turn followed by the voice of John (22.8f.). With 22.10 there begins a new series of words of the angel (22.10f.) and of Jesus (22.12ff.). Perhaps the seer intended 22.15 as a word of his own. An introductory formula, to be sure, is lacking, but the formal and substantial parallelism in the words of Jesus in 22.7 and 12-14 might suggest this understanding of the matter. Both begin with an announcement of the imminent parousia and conclude with a beatitude. This is especially striking in the case of 22.12-14, since the same word is here more richly developed, and since a further member is inserted between the two elements of the double saying. The formal and substantial agreement leads one to suppose that the seer has placed the promise in the mouth of Jesus, but has phrased the threat as a word of his own.

2

As regards content, the two series of sayings are closely linked with the eschatological visions.

The *first angelic word* (22.6) takes up once again the words of 21.5 and confirms them. God, who equips his servants with his prophetic spirit and has shown them 'what will happen soon', stands behind the promise. The word, which already in 1.1 has indicated the content of the book, is apparently here related to the vision of 19.11-22.5.

The *second angelic word* (22.10) is likewise concerned with the prophetic message. It is not to be sealed, but rather to be proclaimed, because the end is close at hand, the time of the great unveiling. But the decision is already being accomplished: 'Now it becomes apparent who is among the just, and who among the wicked.'[262]

Both the *sayings of Jesus* take up the urgent call regarding the imminence of the end: 'And behold, I am coming soon' (22.7,12). For this reason, it is necessary to hold fast to the promise against all temptation. Endurance will not be in vain, for Jesus will come as the divine judge (22.12f.). The formula of deity, which in v.13 is applied to Jesus, links the epilogue with the prologue of the visions of the *eschaton* (21.6). Only the work of those who have accepted the forgiveness of the Lamb (22.14) will stand when the Judge pronounces his verdict. These will have access to the eternal Jerusalem.

John bears witness in his *first word* (22.8f.; cf. 1.4,9) to his prophetic commission and confesses that he, overpowered by the magnitude of what he had experienced, was tempted to worship the mediating angel, but was prevented from doing so (similarly in 19.10).

His *second word* is a variation of the warning which is also expressed in 21.8,27.

Since the epilogue is directed to the church as a promise of salvation and a warning of the judgment, it is in no way surprising that we receive once again — and after 22.3 — a word regarding a threatened exclusion from the realm of salvation in the new Jerusalem.

III

CONCLUSION

In conclusion, let us point out once again a few significant features in the eschatology of John which have to be kept in mind in the interpretation of the entire book.

1. Since, for the seer, the goal of all history has become visible in the history of Jesus, the future will be first of all the unveiling of the true nature of the present. Through the image of the coming one there is proclaimed to the church the salvation that has already appeared here and now.

2. But the salvation, which embraces the whole of created reality, is for the present disclosed only to faith, and so remains a promise for the future.

3. John views the history of revelation from creation to the completion of all things as a history of promise and fulfilment. It is given unity and continuity, not by some innate law, but by the identity of God and his redemptive will in all his acts of revelation.

4. Thus all the Old Testament's images for expressing hope become transparent for John. The mysterious light that permeates them, and causes them to radiate with a lustre never known before, is his faith in the total victory of the Lamb who has been slain, and who through his sacrifice has redeemed mankind from perdition. Because the victory of the Lion of Judah is the victory of the Lamb, because in this way and in no other, Christ is 'King of kings and Lord of lords', there opens up before the seer the prospect of the consummation of his redeeming victory on a universal scale, not only over the church, but also over rejected Israel and, finally, over all creation.

NOTES

Preface

1. So, for instance, R. Bultmann, *Theology of the New Testament*, Vol.II, SCM Press 1955, p.175: 'The Christianity of Revelation has to be termed a weakly Christianized Judaism.'
2. Cf., for instance, P. Althaus, *Die letzten Dinge. Lehrbuch der Eschatologie*, Gütersloher Verlagshaus Gerd Mohn,[8] 1961, pp.297-318.
3. In many religio-historical investigations.
4. In most conservative, harmonizing interpretations.
5. On this point, cf. O. Cullmann, *Salvation in History*, Harper & Row and SCM Press 1967.
6. Cf. the significant article by L. Goppelt, 'Heilsoffenbarung und Geschichte nach der Offenbarung des Johannes', *ThLZ* 77, 9, 1952, cols.513-22 and his *Apostolic and Post-Apostolic Times*, ET, A. and C. Black 1970, pp.111f.; E. Fiorenza, 'The Eschatology and Composition of the Apocalypse', *CBQ* 30, 1968, pp.537-69; K. Karner, 'Gegenwart und Endgeschichte in der Offenbarung des Johannes', *ThLZ* 93, 1968, cols. 641-52.

Introduction

1. Cf. A. Feuillet, *The Apocalypse*, Alba House 1965; G.B. Caird, *The Revelation of St John the Divine*, A. and C. Black 1966, pp.289-301; P.S. Minear, *I Saw a New Earth. An Introduction to the Visions of the Apocalypse*, Corpus Books 1968, pp.201-98. For exegetical details cf. my books: *Time and History. A Study on the Revelation*, John Knox Press 1966; *Alpha und Omega. Eine Deutung der Johannesoffenbarung*, Verlag Friedrich Reinhardt 1966.
2. The question of the genuineness of John's visions is still in debate. Cf. J. Lindblom, *Gesichte und Offenbarungen*, Acta Reg. Societatis Humaniorum Litterarum Lundensis LXV, 1968, pp.206-39.
3. The Old Testament has proved to be of foremost importance for John. He sees the Old Testament promises fulfilled in his message. Cf. A. Schlatter, *Das Alte Testament in der johanneischen Apokalypse*, C. Bertelsmann 1912; E. Lohse, 'Die alttestamentliche Sprache des Sehers Johannes', *ZNW* 52, 1961, pp.122-6; A. Vanhoye, 'L'utilisation du livre d'Ezechiel dans l'Apocalypse', *Biblica* 43, 1962, pp.436-76; A. Lancellotti, 'L'Antico Testimento nell'Apocalisse', *Rivista Biblica* 14, 1966, pp.369-84; L.P. Trüdinger, 'Some Observations Concerning the Text of the Old Testament in the Book of Revelation', *JTS* 17, 1966, pp.82-8. A new discussion of apocalypticism is given by W.R. Murdoch, 'History and Revelation in Jewish Apocalypticism', *Interpr.* 21, 1967, pp.167-87.

4. Cf., e.g., J.A. Bengel, *Erklärte Offenbarung Johannis*, Brodhag'sche Buchhandlung, 1834. A descendant of this species, though a fascinating one, is the book by the nuclear physicist B. Philberth, *Christliche Prophetie und Nuklear Energie*, Christiana-Verlag 1961, who wants to detect in the Apocalypse a minute prefiguration of a possible atomic war.

5. Consult the commentaries of Bousset, Charles, Lohmeyer, Hadorn, Allo, Caird, Farrer, Brütsch; T. Holtz, *Die Christologie der Apokalypse des Johannes*, Akademie-Verlag 1962; J. Comblin, *Le Christ dans l'Apocalypse*, Desclée 1965.

6. This question cannot be dealt with here. Cf., e.g., the discussion by J.N. Sanders, 'St. John on Patmos', *NTS* 9, 1963, pp.75-85.

7. M.E. Boismard, *L'Apocalypse*, Cerf 1950, has attempted to understand the Apocalypse as a combination of two different books by the same author but written at different times. His arguments, however, are inadequate.

8. Cf. W.G. Kümmel, *Introduction to the New Testament*, ET, Abingdon Press and SCM Press 1966, p.34.

9. At any rate, the authors of the Revelation, of the Gospel of John, and of the Johannine letters are different persons.

10. Cf. my books *Time and History. A Study on the Revelation*, pp.75-82, and *Alpha und Omega*, pp.164-74.

11. A. Strobel, 'Abfassung und Geschichtstheologie der Apokalypse nach Kp. 17. 9-12', *NTS* 10, 1964, pp.433-45. Likewise, J. Ernst, *Die eschatologischen Gegenspieler in den Schriften des Neuen Testaments*, Biblische Untersuchungen 3, Verlag F. Pustet 1967, p.157.

12. Cf. T. Holtz, *Die Christologie der Apokalypse des Johannes*, pp.89-109.

13. Cf. my *Time and History*.

14. Cf. W.C. van Unnik, 'A Formula Describing Prophecy', *NTS* 9, 1963, pp.86-94.

15. Cf. esp. L. Goppelt, 'Heilsoffenbarung und Geschichte nach der Offenbarung des Johannes', *ThLZ* 77, 1952, cols.513-22; R. Halver, *Der Mythos im letzten Buch der Bibel*, Herbert Reich-Verlag 1964.

16. Cf. H.J. Kraus, 'Der lebendige Gott', *EvTh* 4, 1967, pp.169-200; J. Bright, *The Kingdom of God*, Abingdon-Cokesbury Press 1953.

17. Also used in Isa. 6.8 and II Kings 22.19ff. Cf. H.P. Müller, 'Die himmlische Ratsversammlung', *ZNW* 54, 1963, pp.254-67.

18. The same combination of these messianic titles in 1Qpatr 1.3f.

19. ἀνοῖξαι (5.5); *inf. finalis* (Charles), or better, *inf. consecutivus* (F. Blass and A. Debrunner, *A Greek Grammar of the New Testament and Other Early Christian Literature*, trans. by R. Funk, University of Chicago Press 1962, 391, 4).

20. This is the primary purpose of the hymns: interpretation of the visions.

21. A good consideration in T. Holtz., op. cit., pp.36-54 and 159-64. The motif of victory is completely misinterpreted by J. Comblin, op. cit., pp.94f., 164ff. His arguments are based on 17.14, which belongs to the secondary insertion.

22. The secondary interpreter of ch.17 (vv.9b-17) has not understood this concept of victory, therefore he speaks of a second, future victory of the Lamb.

23. Cf. the victory formula in the seven messages to the churches in chs.2-3 and 21.7 ($\nu\iota\kappa\tilde{\alpha}\nu$ without object). 12.11: ἐνίκησαν αὐτὸν διὰ τὸ αἷμα τοῦ ἀρνίου.

24. 12.11; 15.2; in contrast to 13.8 ($\nu\iota\kappa\tilde{\alpha}\nu$ with object).

25. This is the thesis of A. Feuillet, 'Le premier Cavalier de l'Apocalypse', *ZNW* 57, 1966, pp.229-59.

26. As the whole image of Antichrist (cf. esp. ch.13) is stamped with the motif of a perverted imitation of Christ, John uses $\nu\iota\kappa\tilde{\alpha}\nu$ without object for Christ *and* Antichrist, but for each in a completely different sense ($\nu\iota\kappa\tilde{\alpha}\nu$ with object; 11.7; 13.7).

27. The basic differences between the victory of Christ and of his antagonist illustrate the particular christological concept of John. The argumentation of Feuillet is not convincing; e.g., the introduction of the bow in 6.2 hardly refers to Ezek. 5.16f. (Feuillet, pp.246f.), for John does not follow in 6.1-8 the pattern of Ezek. 5: neither wild beasts nor 'plague' (ὁ θάνατος linked with ὁ ᾅδης never means 'plague' in Revelation) appear in the scheme of Rev. 6.1-8; the pattern of Ezek. 14.21, however, is applied to the activity of the fourth rider in 6.8. Moreover, the text of Ezek. 5.16f. is in disorder (cf. W. Zimmerli, *Ezechiel*, Biblischer Kommentar, Neukirchener Verlag des Erziehungsvereins 1965, pp.99f., 135f.), and we do not know which text-form John had read or whether the 'arrows' originally formed a special judgment. And even so, we would rather expect the mention of the 'arrows' than the 'bow' in 6.2. Dependence upon Ezekiel, however, is very probable, but the key passage — really speaking of a *bow* as a significant instrument — is, rather, the description of Gog, Ezek. 39.3. I have already drawn attention to the fact that Gog is clearly brought into relationship with the Antichrist figure in Rev. 19.17ff. (Ezek. 39.4,6,17-20; cf. my article 'The Rider on the White Horse', *Interpr.* 18, 1964, pp.407-18). This is a fact, although John applies the mysterious apocalyptic terms 'Gog' and 'Magog' to the bands from the four corners of the earth (20.8)! But here a tradition different from Ezek. 38f. shines through, in which Gog is the name of the sovereign of Magog. 20.8 probably follows a tradition like Ezek. 32.17ff., where — among others — the peoples of Gog appear in the underworld (cf. Ezek. 38.2), for the nations from the four corners of the earth, too, come up out of the underworld (cf. I A). There remain as characteristics in 6.1f. the *crown* of the victor, which is also an attribute of demonic powers in 9.7 (ὡς marks the transposition of the earthly realities into the demonic realm, and the *white colour* of the horse, which can only be understood in the frame of the other form-elements. Because the whole figure of the first rider is clearly antagonistically related to Christ, the white colour is to be interpreted as motif of the Antichrist theme: the first rider wants to appear as the Christ (cf. 19.11ff.). This is the purpose of the Antichrist (cf. 5.6 with 13.3,12,14).

28. Cf. E. Schweizer, 'Die sieben Geister in der Apokalypse', *EvTh* 11,

1951/2, pp.502-12.

29. Cf. 3.10; 6.10; 8.13; 11.10; 13.8,12,14; 17.2,8.

30. We find similar expectations in Jewish apocalyptic circles and, e.g., in II Thess. 2.1ff. Cf. J. Ernst, *Die eschatologischen Gegenspieler in den Schriften des Neuen Testaments* (Biblische Untersuchungen), pp.131-60.

31. οἱ καθημένοι ἐπὶ τῆς γῆς is a variant to οἱ κατοικοῦντες (already in LXX; cf. Jer. 32.15f.).

32. Cf. O. Cullmann, 'Der eschatologische Charakter des Missionsauftrags und des apostolischen Selbstbewusstseins bei Paulus', *Vorträge und Aufsätze 1925-1962*, J.C.B. Mohr 1966, pp.305-36.

33. Cf. 1.3; 2.13,25; 3.8,10; 6.9; 12.17; 14.12; 22.7,9.

34. *Martys* is not yet equated with 'martyr'. The 'witnesses' of Christ are not *martyres* because they die, but they die because they are *martyres* of Christ; cf. N. Brox, *Zeuge und Märtyrer. Untersuchungen zur frühchristlichen Zeugnisterminologie*, Kösel Verlag 1961, pp.92-105; J. Comblin, op. cit., pp.132-63; A. Satake, *Die Gemeindeordnung in der Johannesapokalypse*, Neukirchener Verlag 1966, pp.119-33.

35. 2.9; 3.9; 6.10; 16.6; 17.6; 18.23f.; 19.2.

36. T. Holtz, *op. cit.*, pp.118-21.

37. Cf. S. Brown, 'The Hour of Trial', *JBL* 85, 1966, pp.308-14.

38. This seems to me the best interpretation of Harmagedon = *harmoed*; cf. J. Jeremias, 'Harmagedon', *ZNW* 31, 1932, p.205.

39. The considerations on the state of the dead in the Revelation by K. Hanhart, *The Intermediate State in the New Testament* (doctoral dissertation, University of Amsterdam, Groningen, 1966), pp.224-33, are too vague.

40. Cf. my article, 'Das Judenproblem im Lichte der Johannes-Apokalypse', *ThZ* 13, 1957, pp.241-59.

Chapters I and II

1. It is a traditional feature in the Jewish apocalypses since Ezekiel. Cf. Minear, *I Saw a New Earth*, p.161.

2. We find the same scheme also in Rev. 4.4 (the twenty-four thrones and the elders); 20.4 (the thrones and those who share in the millennium); 6.2-8 (the horses and the rider).

3. Acts 1.9,11; Mark 13.26 par.; I Thess. 4.17. The concept is based upon Dan. 7.13 where 'one like a son of man' appears 'with the clouds of heaven'; cf. R.B.Y. Scott, 'Behold, He Cometh with Clouds', *NTS* 5, 1959, pp.127-32.

4. The white horse is hardly a reminder of the cloud of the parousia.

5. Compare the white garments of the heavenly beings, the white throne of God; on this point cf. W. Michaelis, *TDNT* IV, pp.241-50.

6. On the significance of his counter image, the Antichrist who rides on the white horse in 6.1f., cf. my article 'The Rider on the White Horse', *Interpr.* 18, 1964, pp.407-18.

7. This betrays the typical style of the Semite who is not interested in the external appearance of a person but in the dynamism of his characteristics and functions, as T. Boman, *Hebrew Thought Compared with Greek*, Westminster Press and SCM Press 1960, pp.76-89, has very ably shown.

8. W. Bousset, *Die Offenbarung Johannis*, KEK, Vandenhoeck & Ruprecht 1906, p.431, eventually wished to omit the Logos name as the 'idle fancy' of a copyist; so also J. Wellhausen, *Analyse der Offenbarung Johannis*, Weidmann 1907, p.30.

9. E. Lohmeyer, *Die Offenbarung des Johannes, Handbuch zum NT* 16, J.C.B. Mohr, ^{2}1953, p.159, has rightly recognized that the statement in v.11 'is related to the believers, the second (name, v.16) to the "world"'. However, it is not clear why just in the Logos name 'beide ihren Herrn verehren und sein eigentümliches Wesen erkennen'. See further below.

10. Rev. 1.4,12-20; 2-3; 4.5; 5.6. Because the Lord of history is none other than the Lord of the church, the number seven is also transferred to the chaotic end of history as a principle of order in the sevenfold series of visions of the end-time. Cf. my book *Time and History*.

11. Rev. 4.6 (the four beings as representatives of creation; cf. W. Zimmerli, *Ezechiel*, p.53); 7.1 (the four winds from the four corners of the earth: an image of the all-embracing eschatological tribulation); similarly 9.15.

12. The position of καλούμενος between the two notions in S is to be explained with J. Schmid, *Studien zur Geschichte des griechischen Apokalypse-Textes*, 2, K. Zink, 1955, p.130: 'S hat das in A, Andreas-Kommentar, fehlende καλούμενος erst nach K erganzt.' K and Origen certainly are witnesses here to the certainty of the original text.

13. Rev. 19.9 is apparently also to be understood in this way, since ἀληθινοί is likewise linked here with the words of promise. ἀληθινός takes on a different colour in connection with δίκαιος associated with the ways and judgment of God: 15.13; 16.7; 19.2.

14. Rev. 1.2,9; 6.9; 12.17; 19.10. Reference is always to the testimony given by Jesus (subjective genitive). For this reason John can speak of ἔχειν it (6.9; 19.10). This message determines the life of believers. Where it is held fast to and also proclaimed as 'their message' (11.7; 12.11) it provokes resistance.

15. Rev. 22.6,7; 1.2f. The introductory words of Rev. 1.1 are based upon Hos. 1.1 ('the word of the Lord that came to Hosea'). The nature of the word of Jesus which is received is described as ἀποκάλυψις, the unveiling of the secret of the end-time and of the perfection. Lohmeyer's interpretation (see n.9) of it as a timeless revelation, uncircumscribed as to time and content (p.7), does not at all correspond to the content of our book.

16. Cf. my book *Time and History*.

17. John reads *amen*, not *omen*. We find emphasis placed upon the faithfulness of God also in Exod. 34.6; Ps. 86.15; cf. III Macc. 2.11; II Cor. 1.20.

18. So correctly A. Wikenhauser, *Die Offenbarung des Johannes*,

Verlag Friedrich Pustet, 1947, p.44. In 3.14, Ps. 89.28,38 is used as in
Rev. 1.5. Jesus' words are valid and trustworthy as the words of 'the
witness' and 'the Amen' (1.5; 2.13; 3.14) who reveals the word of God
which is given to him by God himself (1.1); cf. K. Berger, *Die Amen-
Worte Jesu* , BZNW 39, 1970, pp.106ff. and my book *Das Evangelium des
Johannes. Kommentar zum Neuen Testament,* R. Brockhaus Verlag 1972
(on John 1.51).

19. Cf. T. Holtz, *Die Christologie der Apokalypse des Johannes*, p.143.
Holtz, however, recognizes the difficulty of this interpretation: this
would be 'the only passage in the whole complex of the Christ-vision
1.12ff. and the messages to the churches where a reference is made to the
history of Christ'.

20. The church, too, is a witness as a bearer of this prophetic message of
Jesus. Thus the two witnesses who as such 'speak prophetically' in
Jerusalem (11.3). This and not their death makes them 'witnesses'. 11.3-7
and 1.1-6 also show that we cannot separate μάρτυς, μαρτυρία, μαρτυρεῖν
from one another. Thus John himself witnesses his message (1.2), the
church 'keeps' it, in that she passes it on in the readiness to pay for it with
her life (Antipas 2.13; 6.9; 12.11; 17.6; 20.4). Comparison of 17.6
('blood of the saints and the witnesses') with 18.24 ('blood of the
prophets and the saints') might suggest an identification of the witnesses
and prophets, but it cannot be proved with certainty. At any rate, the
witness is not necessarily a martyr (cf. N. Brox, *Zeuge und Märtyrer,*
pp.92-105). Brox says rightly on 11.7: 'Die Zeit ihrer μαρτυρία ist die Zeit
ihrer Unantastbarkeit, sodass das Wort genau das meint, was *vor* ihrem
Martyrium liegt.'

21. Nowhere in the New Testament (cf. Rom. 8.29; Col. 1.15,18; Heb.
1.6).

22. Holtz (see n.19), pp.57f.

23. Ibid., p.169.

24. V. Herntrich, *TDNT* III, 1965, pp.929-33; Holtz (see n.19), p.170.

25. In 2.16, probably referring to a judgment which occurs within
history. Holtz, p.170, also points to the image of a holy war of God
against his own people in Amos 2.14-16.

26. Holtz, p.171.

27. Borrowing from key passage Dan. 10.6 (Rev. 1.14). It is not certain
whether we have to read ὡς in 19.12 as in 1.14; cf. Schmid (see n.12),
pp.93,226.

28. Holtz, p.122, rightly points to the correspondence of this introductory word with 2.23 in the same message to the churches (cf. Ps. 7.10;
Jer. 11.20; 17.10).

29. On this point cf. especially G. Bornkamm, 'Die Komposition der
apokalyptischen Visionen in der Offenbarung Johannis', *Studien zu
Antike und Urchristentum* 2, 1959, pp.204-22.

30. The diadem is 'a sign of personal sovereignty without reference to
definite territory': R. Delbrueck, 'Antiquarisches zu den Verspottungen
Jesu', *ZNW* 41, 1942, p.143. Delbrueck's attempt to derive the image of
Christ from Ptolemaeus VI Philometor (I Macc. 11.13), who wore two

diadems, cannot be proved (pp.143f.). John stresses the absolutely unusual concentration of power in the figures of the dragon, Antichrist, and — exceeding all — of Christ.

31. ἔχων, participle instead of *verbum finitum* as in 10.2; 12.2; 21.12,14.

32. ὄνομα βλασφημίας is well testified to by P 47 SCP Andreas-Comm. The plural could be a secondary assimilation to 17.3.

33. Cf. H. Bietenhard, *TDNT* V, 1967, pp.242ff.

34. R.H. Charles, *The Revelation of St John*, ICC, Scribner and T.& T. Clark 1920, Vol.II, pp.115,132, for instance, thinks of *Kyrios* or the *Tetragrammaton*. He prefers, however, to excise the statement as a gloss. M. Rist, 'The Revelation of St John', *Interpreter's Bible*, Abingdon 1957, p.513, thinks of the name of Jesus. O. Cullmann, *The Christology of the New Testament*, SCM Press and Westminster Press 1963, p.314, is probably closer to the truth when he suggests the name of God. Already in the Old Testament God gives new names which are expressions of the new nature or the new situation of their bearers (Gen. 17.5,17; 32.28f.; 35.10; Isa. 65.15; 62.2; Zech. 8.3); cf. Bietenhard, *TDNT* V, 1967, p.254. Among the six realities which would be renewed in the end-time, Judaism mentions the name of the Messiah.

35. Charles (see n.34), p.133, seeks to support himself by referring to the blood of the Parthian king and his armies 'whom he had already destroyed and whose destruction had already been proleptically prophesied in 17.14'. Lohmeyer (see n.9), p.159, even rules out all questions concerning the victory and the enemies. The garment is, according to him, simply a symbol of victory even before the battle begins. But such arguments are not convincing. G.B. Caird, *Comm.*, p.243, wants to find here 'the indelible traces of the death of his followers'.

36. A. Schlatter, *Das Alte Testament in der johanneischen Apokalypse*, p.47; C. Brütsch, *Clarté de l'Apocalypse*, Labor et Fides 1955, p.188; R.H. Preston and A.T. Hanson, *The Revelation of St John*, Torch Bible Commentaries, SCM Press 1957, p.120 also interpret in the same way.

37. Rev. 7.14 shows that the image of the dipping of a garment in blood is not foreign to John.

38. Excellently testified to by A Andreas-Comm., K, sa, sy[1].

39. S bo latt Oik Hipp. Orig. Schmid (see n.12), p.114, rightly emphasizes that περιφεραμμένον cannot be merely a scribal error.

40. Rev. 12.5; 5.5; 1.5,18; 11.8. Cf. my book cited in n.10.

41. In the Synoptic Apocalypse the parousia of the Son of Man is also connected first of all with the gathering of the elect, Mark 13.26f.; cf. I Cor. 15.23; I Thess. 4.16f.

42. The double aspect of the eschatological event is to be found throughout the Revelation of John; cf. the hymns in 19.1-3 (judgment), 4-9 (the marriage of the Lamb), 14.14-16 (assembling of the elect), 17-20 (judgment of the nations), 11.15-18 (judgment), 19 (sign of the grace of the covenant).

43. Holtz, pp.127,178f., with good reason rejects any combination of the Logos title in v.12 with the sword issuing from the mouth and the idea

of a martial word of God (Wisd. of Sol. 18.15) or with the eschatological sword of God. Our investigation confirms his conclusion.

44. Quoted according to the Septuagint, which reflects a different Hebrew original; cf. J. Jeremias, *TDNT* VI, 1968, p.494, n.87.

45. Cf. 14.10; 16.19 (Isa. 51.17). The clarity of the image suffers from this, but John likes such allusions to the Old Testament; cf. E. Lohse, 'Die alttestamentliche Sprache des Sehers Johannes', *ZNW* 52, 1961, pp.122-6.

46. Deut. 9.17; cf. Dan. 2.47; Ps. 136.2f. With regard to the Jewish titles, cf. W. Bousset & H. Gressmann, *Die Religion des Judentums im späthellenistischen Zeitalter*, J.C.B. Mohr 1926, p.313.

47. Cf. I Tim. 6.15. The fact that the name appears not only on the coat but also on the thigh has given rise to much guessing. Wellhausen (see n.8), p.30, reads ἵππον instead of ἱμάτιον: 'so that the genitive αὐτοῦ behind μηρόν can be related to the horse.' C.S. Torrey, 'Studies in the Aramaic of the First Century AD', *ZNW* 65, 1954, p.235, who believes in a Greek translation of the book out of a Semitic original, thinks of a confusion of the words for 'his banner' and 'his leg.' This feature cannot be explained with certainty; cf., however, J.J. Wettstein, *Prolegomena in Novum Testamentum*, 2, 1752, and Lohmeyer (see n.9). Scholars have pointed to the thigh as a place of the sword (Judg. 3.16; Ps. 45.8) or the seat of procreative power (Gen. 24.2; etc.), but I could find only one real analogy in the text of 4QMess ar (cf. J.A. Fitzmyer, 'The Aramaic "Elect of God" Text from Qumran Cave IV', *CBQ* 27, 1965, pp.348-72, which speaks in col. 1.3 of 'Tiny Marks on His Thigh' (of the Messiah). But we do not know what this remark means.

48. On this point, cf. my article cited in n.6.

49. On this point, cf. H. Bietenhard, *Das tausendjährige Reich*, Beg Verlag 1944.

50. ἀνοῖξαι τὸ βιβλίον is an infinite of result (F. Blass and A. Debrunner, *A Greek Grammar of the New Testament*, trans. by R. Funk, 391,4). Cf. the interpreting hymn in 5.9f. On the whole image, cf. H.P. Müller, 'Die himmlische Ratsversammlung, Motivgeschichtliches zu Apk. 5.1-5', *ZNW* 54, 1963, pp.254-67.

51. The opinion of Wellhausen (see n.8), p.30, which is shared by almost all commentators, completely misses the point: '19.11-21 leaps from the triumph back to the battle.' The use of νικᾶν without the object appears not only in 5.5 but also in 6.2 in a description of the Antichrist (cf. my article cited in n.6). But the difference in the tense clearly distinguishes the victory of the Lamb which is obtained once and for all (ἐνίκησεν) from the imperfect 'victory' of the adversary which will never reach its goal (νικῶν καὶ ἵνα νικήσῃ).

52. To this belongs also 13.18 and the mention of the number of the name in 15.2.

53. Rev. 1.5; 6.15; 18.3,9; 19.19; 21.24; also in the original text of ch.17 (vv.2 and 18!).

54. Cf. especially K. Karner, 'Gegenwart und Endgeschichte in der Offenbarung des Johannes', *ThLZ* 93, 1968, col.652: '. . . dass in der

Vollendung als offene und unwidersprochene Realität zutage tritt, was schon jetzt als eschatologische Wirklichkeit unter der Herrschaft des Lammes verborgen besteht.'

55. R.H. Charles, *The Revelation of St John*, ICC, 1920, Vol.II, pp.144ff. He has the heavenly Jerusalem after 20.3 and arranges the text as follows: 20.1-3; 21.9-22,2,14,15,17; 20.4-6,7-10,11-15; 21.5a,4d,5b, 1-4abc; 22.3-5; 21.5c,6b-8; 22.6-7,18a,16,13,12,10,8,9,20,21. A new arrangement of the text again has been attempted by P. Gaechter, 'The Original Sequence of Apocalypse 20-22', *Theological Studies* 10, 1949, pp.485-521, and E. Boismard, 'L'Apocalypse ou les Apocalypses de St. Jean', *RB* 56, 1949, pp.507-41. Such a *tour de force* should really be attempted only if absolutely certain indications of textual confusion are present, which is not the case here.

56. *The Revelation of St John*, Vol.II, p.144.

57. E. Lohmeyer, *Die Offenbarung des Johannes*, p.161, thinks that more strongly 'traditional material is, so to speak, rather presented here without the peculiar concepts of the seer being especially to the fore'; p.163: 'Thus, through the mouth of the seer there speaks a tradition which has been taken over, as it were, in order to give the report completeness.'

58. Cf. I A, 2.

59. On Ticonius' and Augustine's influential interpretations, cf. W. Bousset, *Die Offenbarung Johannis*, KEK, pp.56ff.

60. It is in accord with the style of John that the thrones are seen first of all, after which the seer speaks of sitting on them, and then finally describes those who sit. In the same way in 4.2 we find a description of the throne, then the statement that someone is sitting on it, and only then a description of the appearance of the one who is enthroned (the omission of καὶ ὁ καθήμενος 4.3 [Andrew Comm. K against ASP 1611 2050 2329] is a correction; cf. J. Schmid, *Studien zur Geschichte des griechischen Apokalypse-Textes*, 2, p.75).

61. Lohmeyer and others think only of the one group of martyrs; there is no reason to omit οἵτινες with Charles. Reflections about members of the community of the last generation who are still alive and their transformation in the sense of I Cor. 15.51f., are absent. The seer perhaps expects, according to 13.17 and 11. 7, the physical destruction of the whole church with the result that the whole church is among the dead at the time of the parousia.

62. MT:ממלכת בהנים LXX; βασίλειον ἱεράτευμα.

63. It is not entirely certain which variant is original, βασιλεύσουσιν or βασιλεύουσιν; but probably the future reading (as a promise related to the present, since the statement is a part of the characterization of the destiny of the church in the present introduced by ἐποίησεν).

64. Hugo Gressmann, *Altorientalische Texte zum Alten Testament*, Walter de Gruyter 1926, pp.206f., 320-22.

65. Cf. Bundehesh 3.26; 13.77.

66. Cf. C. Barth, *Die Errettung vom Tode in den individuellen Klage- und Dankliedern des Alten Testaments*, Evangelischer Verlag Zollikon

1947, p.78.

67. In Jewish apocalypticism: Ethiopian Enoch 10.4-10; 18.12-19.1; 21.1-6; Test. Lev. 18.2. Regarding 'sealing' as a sign of locking up, cf. Prayer of Manasseh 3f.; Od. Sol. 24.7.

68. God and Christ do not act; the dragon is chained by an angel (cf. also ch.12). Regarding the significance of this motif for the seer's eschatology, cf. I A, 3.

69. δεῖ 20.3 points to the fact that these events are a part of God's plan of redemption; cf. 1.1,19; 10.7; Dan. 2.28f.,45; cf. E. Fascher, 'Theologische Betrachtungen zu δεῖ', *ZNW* 21, 1954, pp.228-54, esp. 253.

70. On all problems of detail cf. H. Bietenhard, *Das tausendjährige Reich*, 1944. Basically John follows the pattern of Ezek. 37-48: resurrection and messianic kingdom (Ezek. 37) — Gog/Magog and their destruction (Ezek. 38f.) — the Holy City and its temple (Ezek. 40-46) — the Holy Land (Ezek. 47f.). It is obvious that the concept of the millennium has no place in Paul's eschatological terminology (cf. H.W. Wilcke, *Das Problem eines messianischen Zwischenreichs bei Paulus*, Zwingli-Verlag 1967, but note that the notion 'Zwischenreich' does not really apply to John's conception!).

71. O. Cullmann, 'The Kingship of Christ and the Church in the New Testament', in: *The Early Church*, SCM Press 1956, p.113 [translation mine].

72. On ἔζησαν as an expression for the resurrection, cf. Rom. 14.9: ἔζησεν used of the resurrection of Jesus (and exactly so in Rev. 2.8; and of the Antichrist's imitation of the resurrection in 13.14). John quite probably alludes to Ezek. 27.10.

73. The words καὶ κρίμα ἐδόθη αὐτοῖς are also certainly to be understood in the light of the notions of 'throne' and 'ruling', for the Old Testament שפט embraces both meanings, 'ruling' and 'judging', which were taken over by the Septuagint. In the New Testament: Matt. 19.28; Luke 22.30. The expression is taken over from Dan. 7.22 (cf. Wisd. 3.8), where it is an equivalent for ודינא יהיב . This is probably what John thought of here.

74. Against C.H. Brütsch, *Die Offenbarung Jesu Christi*, Zürcher Bibelkommentare, 1970, Vol.II, p.338.

75. Charles, op. cit., Vol.II, p.186; W. Hadorn, *Die Offenbarung des Johannes*, Theologischer Handkommentar zum NT, Evangelische Verlagsanstalt 1928, p.196.

76. Only in 11.3ff. does John speak of the proclamation of the church to the world. In the rest of the book he emphasizes only the keeping of the word, since the word is chiefly seen as a sign of election, the possession of which makes the church the church (cf. ἔχειν of the word in 6.9; cf. 1.3,9; 12.17; 14.12). The gospel stands here in the place of the law in Jewish apocalypticism; cf. D. Rössler, *Gesetz und Geschichte*, Neukirchener Verlag 1960, pp.77ff.

77. Charles, op. cit., Vol.II, p.143.

78. Thus ἀπαρχή is to be understood as first-fruits in relation to the whole of mankind (14.4).

79. Undoubtedly stemming originally from apocalyptic week-speculations, which Revelation characteristically does not take over, the number
has become the sign of the messianic time, just as the three and a half
times of Daniel has become the sign of the end-time. The number 1000
qualifies the *moment* when history comes to an end as the moment of the
perfect revelation of Christ's lordship over the world. P.S. Minear, op. cit.,
pp.175-9, rightly emphasizes the problem of this 'time' concept which
transcends chronology.

80. Cf. with this the careful considerations of W. Michaelis, *Versöhnung des Alls*, Siloah-Verlag 1950, pp.97-121. 'Death' refers in Revelation
not merely to physical annihilation but rather to a judgment which goes
on even after death. The believers take part in the 'first death', insofar as
they too must die and must bear the awesome sign of belonging to the old
sinful world. But their death is not entrance into judgment but into the
heavenly sanctuary (7.9-17; 15.2-4), where they wait for the annihilation
of all that is temporary. Therefore, those who die in the Lord are blessed
(14.13). The 'second death', however, is the event of eschatological
judgment which again does not refer to annihilation but to unending pain.
The redeemed are freed from this by the deed of Jesus. In rabbinic
Judaism the second death means exclusion from the resurrection or
eternal condemnation; on this point cf. H.L. Strack-P. Billerbeck, *Kommentar zum Neuen Testament aus Talmud und Midrasch* III, C.H. Beck
1926, pp.830f.; cf. II B e, 3.

81. Cf. n.57.

82. See A. Bertholet, 'Zu den babylonischen und israelitischen Unter-
weltsvorstellungen', *Oriental Studies*, 1926, pp.10ff.; C. Barth, *Die
Errettung vom Tode in den individuellen Klage- und Dankliedern des
Alten Testaments*, EVZ, 1947, pp.76ff.; P. Reymond, *L'eau, sa vie, et sa
signification dans l'Ancien Testament*, E.J. Brill 1958, pp.212-4; A.J.
Wensinck, *The Ocean in the Literature of the Western Semites*, J. Muller
1918.

83. Cf. C. Barth, op. cit., p.83: 'Fern von der Lebenswelt könnte das
Totenreich auch sein, ohne gerade in der Tiefe zu liegen. Um dies
auszudrücken, würde der Name fernes Land (*ki-sud, kur-sud, ersitu rûqtu,
ki-bad, nisâti*) oder der von den Ägyptern gebrauchte Euphemismus
"dort" genugen.' The Revelation knows several different 'entrances' to
the underworld (cf. 9.1f.; 13.1).

84. C. Barth, p.83.

85. Cf. S. Mowinckel, *Psalmenstudien II*, Jacob Dybwad 1961,
pp.261-3.

86. The expression is certainly related to Ezek. 38.11f., since the whole
imagery in Rev. 20.7-10 is influenced by Ezekiel. However, it remains
'iridescent' (Lohmeyer) and without any specific geographic reference
(cf. my article in *ThZ* 13, 1957, pp.241ff.; J.J. Stamm, *Der Staat Israel
und die Landverheissungen der Bibel*, 1957, pp.34ff.; F.C. Fensham,
' "Camp" in the New Testament and Milchama', *Revue de Qumran* 4/16,
1964, pp.557-62).

87. At the four corners of the earth there are also the angels of the

eschatological winds (7.1; cf. Dan. 7.2). πλανῆσαι is used here concretely as in 13.14 of seduction to a particular course of action.

88. According to Ezek. 38f. Gog is the last enemy of God's people who comes from the land of Magog. But the Septuagint has already translated ἐπὶ Γωγ καὶ τὴν γῆν τοῦ Μαγωγ. In Jewish traditions both appear as names of nations at enmity with God. The assumption that John could have thought here of the inhabitants of the underworld is also made by W. Metzger ('Das Zwischenreich', in *Festschrift für Bischof T. Wurm. Auf dem Grunde der Apostel und Propheten,* ed. *M. Loeser, 1948,* pp.100-118), but without seeing the internal relationships of the whole conception. He rightly points to Ezek. 32.17ff. where many nations appear in the kingdom of the dead, among them even the nations of Gog of Ezek. 38.2, Mesech and Tubal! The term 'nations' is no argument against our interpretation (as C.H. Brütsch [see n.74], Vol.III, p.362, thinks), because terms like 'kings' and 'armies' can also refer to men *or* demons and John thinks here first of all of 'the dead' in the underworld (1.18; 6.8). Their appearance in the last attempt to conquer the people of God reveals their powerlessness, and their appearance in the Last Judgment (20.11ff.) their guilt.

89. So also in the whole section 19.11-20. Cf. I A, 3. The Jewish idea of a messianic war in which the people of God are engaged (cf. esp. the Scroll of War of Qumran) has no place in the expectations of Revelation.

90. Cf. W. Michaelis, *TDNT* IV, pp.241-50. The white throne is perhaps thought of as identical with the throne of 4.1.

91. I cannot see in it a weakness of John's theology 'dass sie nicht die Kraft hat, die im Verborgenen, ja im Gegenteil dennoch wirkliche Sieger- und Herrscherstellung des Christus und der Glieder seiner Gemeinde bis an das Ende in solcher Verhüllung zu belassen, bis sie aufgehoben ist in dem neuen Aeon, sondern eine Zeit ihrer Darstellung auch in diesem Aeon erwartet' (so F. Holtz, *Die Christologie der Apokalypse des Johannes,* Akademie-Verlag 1962, p.183), but rather something of the faithfulness of God toward this earth, which is witnessed to in the Old Testament.

92. Cf. esp. C. Barth, op. cit., pp.76-91.

93. Parallels: Syr. Bar. 24.1; Ps. Philo, *Antt.* 3.10; En. 89.61ff.; 97.6; 98.7f.; Sl. Enoch 52.15. It would, of course, be possible to understand the 'works' in a neutral sense; there would then be nothing about a differentiation on the basis of works, and the book of life would in any case still be decisive.

94. Regarding the heavenly book with the names of the redeemed, cf. Exod. 33.32; Ps. 69.29 (book of the living, of the Jews); Enoch 47.3; Phil. 4.3 (book of life); Luke 10.20; Heb. 12.23.

95. The comparison between the eschatology of John and the Revelation undertaken by L. van Hartingsveld, *Die Eschatologie des Johannes-evangeliums,* Van Gorcum 1962, pp.180-85, on the basis of a comparison of concepts, is too superficial because he does not do justice to the intentions behind the apocalyptic concepts.

96. Cf. esp. the investigations of L. Kitschelt, *Die frühchristliche Basilika als Darstellung des himmlischen Jerusalem,* 1938, and H. Sedl-

mayer, *Die Entstehung der Kathedrale*, Atlantis-Verlag 1950. Even if the idea of 'city' is not the original basic concept of the early Christian basilica (cf. W. Rordorf, 'Was wissen wir über die christlichen Gottesdiensträume der vorkonstantinischen Zeit?', *ZNW* 55, 1964, p.127), it certainly is in the later interpretation, and it forms the dominating factor in the shaping of the medieval cathedral.

97. The trend toward the identification of the holy city and the church already begins with the apologists. Origen mentions 'the city of the great king, the true Jerusalem, *or* the church, built out of living stones' (commentary on John 4.19f.). Further evidence in K.L. Schmidt, *Die Polis in Kirche und Welt* (Rektoratsprogramm der Universität Basel), F. Reinhardt 1939, pp.68f. It is interesting how Cyril of Jerusalem in his 18th Baptismal Catechesis (18,26) shifts the origin of the earthly church completely to the earth in that, alluding to Gal. 4.26, he calls the earthly church and not the heavenly Jerusalem 'the mother of us all', 'the copy of the heavenly Jerusalem which is the free mother of us all.' Although Augustine distinguished the coming kingdom of God from the time of the church, he too calls the church already the *regnum Christi regnumque caelorum (De civitate Dei* 20, 9). The heavenly Jerusalem is descending from heaven since its beginning: *de caelo quidem ab initio descendit, ex quo per huius saeculi tempus gratia Dei desuper veniente per lavacrum regenerationis in Spiritu sancto misso de caelo subinde cives eius adcrescunt (De civ.* 20, 17).

99. H. Schlier, *Der Brief an die Galater*, KEK, Vandenhoeck & Ruprecht 1949, p.159. Cf. the peculiar shift from a spatial contrast to a temporal one: the 'heavenly' Jerusalem opposed to the 'present' Jerusalem (Gal. 4.25f.).

100. Cf. n.99. On the transference of the temple motif to the community in Qumran and in the NT, cf. F. Gärtner, *The Temple and the Community in Qumran and the New Testament*, Cambridge University Press 1965.

101. P. Bonnard, *L'Épître de Saint Paul aux Galates*, Commentaire du N.T.9, Delachaux & Niestlé 1953, p.98.

102. Cf. esp. O. Michel, *Der Brief an die Hebraer*, KEK, 1949, p.350.

103. A. Alt, 'Jerusalems Aufstieg', in *Kleine Schriften zur Geschichte des Volkes Israel*, Vol.III, C.H. Beck 1959, p.247; on the geography and history cf. J. Simons, *Jerusalem in the Old Testament*, Brill 1952, and P.L.H. Vincent, *Jerusalem de l'Ancien Testament*, J. Gabalda 1954/56.

104. Cf. M. Noth, 'Jerusalem und die israelitische Tradition', in *Gesammelte Studien zum A.T.*, C. Kaiser 1957, pp.172-87.

105. Isa. 48.2; 52.1; 66.20; Neh. 11.1; Dan. 9.24; I Macc. 2.7; II Macc. 1.12; 3.1; 9.14; Josephus, *Antt.* 4.70; 20.118, etc.

106. Isa. 2.3; Micah 4.2; Isa. 66.20; 27.13.

107. G. von Rad, 'The City on the Hill', in *The Problem of the Hexateuch and other Essays*, Oliver and Boyd 1966, pp.232-42, has pursued the same motif in Isa. 2.1-4; Isa. 60; Hagg. 2.6-9ff.; the quotation comes from p.234.

108. Cf. n.107.

109. The reference to the reports about the application of lapis lazuli and malachite as adornment of an Egyptian palace (P. Volz, *Jesaja II* [Komm. zum. A.T.] , A. Deichert 1932, p.137 — according to Erman, *Ägypten* I, 1885, p.259) can hardly suffice for an interpretation of the whole concept. Perhaps, rather, an astromythological concept of a heavenly city built out of stars lies behind these ideas.

110. 'The house of Yahweh' (Isa. 2.2) is Jerusalem, not the temple, as the context shows (v.3).

111. M. Schmidt, *Prophet und Tempel. Eine Studie zum Problem der Gottesnähe im A.T.*, Evangelischer Verlag Zollikon 1948, p.161; cf. also pp.129ff., concerning Ezek. 40-48, esp. pp.163-71.

112. Cf. Ezek. 20.44; 36.22-8; 37.

113. Ezek. 36.25; cf. also Zech. 13.1.

114. Ezek. 36.26; cf. Jer. 31.31-40.

115. Ezek. 43.7; 48.35; 37.27.

116. The nations are also included in Ezek. 37.26-8; cf. Isa. 40.5; 42.6; 49.6; 51.4f.; 52.10; 54.20-22; 55.5; 62.10f.; Zech. 2.11-13; Ps. 96.3,10.

117. The basic motifs are shaped in different ways; in part, the nations serve for the glorification of Jerusalem, or the greatness of the revelation of glory is indicated by the greatness of their gifts, and the journey of the nations to Jerusalem leads to general worship of Yahweh; cf. Micah 7.11f.; Isa. 18.7; 45.14,23f.; 56.6f.; 66.18-20; Jer. 3.17; 16.19; Zeph. 3.9f.; Zech. 14.16; Hagg. 2.7-9; Ps. 22.28f.; 47; 68.30,32f.; 86.9; 72.10f.; 96.7f.

118. 'Tower' is also a name for the Temple in Eth. Enoch 89.50,54,56,66f.,73.

119. The texts are collected by Strack-Billerbeck, op. cit. (see n.80), pp.849f. and Vol.IV, 2, 1928, pp.883ff.

120. Ibid., Vol.IV, 1, p.213; cf. Ecclus. 36.18f. and the third benediction in the grace at the table: 'Build Jerusalem, the holy city, speedily in our days! Blessed be thou, Yahweh, who builds Jerusalem in his mercy' (ibid., Vol.IV 2, p.631).

121. Cf. P. Volz, *Die Eschatologie der jüdischen Gemeinde im neutestamentlichen Zeitalter*, J.C.B. Mohr 1934, p.373. Perhaps the concepts of the new temple and the new Jerusalem flow into one another here (H. Bietenhard, *Die himmlische Welt im Urchristentum und Spätjudentum*, J.C.B. Mohr 1951, p.195).

122. The name of Jerusalem appears in this sense: 1QpHab IX, 4f.; XII, 7ff.; 1Qi4 fragm. 8-10 and 11,13 (uncertain reading); 4QpIs^b II, 7.10; 4QpIs^c 11; 4QpNah 2.11; 4Qtest 30.

123. Text by J.M. Allegro, *JBL* 77, 1958, pp.215-21; 4QpIs^d on pp.220f. But cf. the corrections by Y. Yadin, *Israel Exploration Journal* 9, 1959, pp.39-45.

124. The meaning of this expression is disputed.

125. The War Scroll seems to deal with a future eschatological war. The 'realistic' traits in the description of the army and the battle, which are probably taken over from a *Vorlage*, serve to make the image concrete. Cf. to this J. Hempel, *Die Texte von Qumran in der heutigen Forschung*,

Nachrichten der Akademie der Wissenschaften in Gottingen, I, Philologisch-historische Klasse, Vandenhoeck & Ruprecht 1961, pp.309-11.

126. Published by J.M. Allegro, *JBL* 75, 1956, pp.177-82.

127. Cf. A.S. van der Woude, *Die messianischen Vorstellungen der Gemeinde von Qumran*, Van Gorcum 1957, pp.179ff. The leader of the enemies stretches out his 'hand against the mountain of the daughter of Zion, against the hill of Jerusalem' (cf. also line 11).

128. In the first fragment of the commentary of Isaiah we find in line 1 the same report on the situation as in 1QM I, 3:'. . . [with]the [return] from the wilderness of the nations . . .'

129. Cf. J. Maier, *Die Texte vom toten Meer*, Vol. II, E. Reinhardt 1960, p.112.

130. M. Baillet, 'Fragments araméens de Qumran 2, description de la Jerusalem nouvelle', *RB* 62, 1955, pp.222-45; on this cf. J. Starcky, *RB* 63, 1956, p.66 and J.T. Milik, *RB* 63, pp.55f.; J. Hempel, *Die Texte von Qumran in der heutigen Forschung*, pp.324f.

131. The fragments speak of prophetic visions (cf. fragm. 1,11,15,17; 8,7; perhaps also 9,2). The visionary temple is therefore to be understood as a futuristic entity. This does not exclude the possibility that the liturgies of the angels of 4QSI know also of a heavenly temple and worship (published by J. Strugnell, Suppl. *VT* 7, 1960, pp.318ff.); cf. M. Hengel, *Judentum und Hellenismus*, J.C.B. Mohr 1969, pp.404f.

132. The Septuagint already adds to the image of the new Jerusalem in Isa. 54.15: ἰδοὺ προσήλυτοι προσελεύσονταί σοι δι'ἐμοῦ (cf. also LXX Amos 9.12); Tobit 13.13; 3 Sib. 716ff.,725f.,772-5; Test. Ben. 9.2; Eth. Enoch 10.21; 48.5; 53.1.; 90.33; Syr. Bar. 68,5; Ps. Sal. 17.31; 4 Esr. 13.12f.; on the rabbinic texts, Strack-Billerbeck, Vol. III, pp.150-52.

133. Ibid., pp.144f.,150-55.

134. The texts are collected in ibid., p.573.

135. For the later witnesses, cf. H. Bietenhard, op. cit., pp.194f.

136. H. Bietenhard (see n.121), p.195.

137. Slav. Enoch 55.2 and Test. Dan. 5.12 betray a similar conception. Whether some Qumran circles believed in the immortality of the soul and a heavenly paradise is hard to determine because of our fragmentary knowledge of the Qumran eschatology; cf. J. van der Ploeg, 'L'immortalité de l'homme d'après les textes de la Mer Morte', *VT* 2, 1952, pp.171-5.

138. E. Lohse, *Die Offenbarung des Johannes*, Das Neue Testament Deutsch, Vandenhoeck und Ruprecht 1960, p.101.

139. H. Strathmann, *TDNT* VI, p.532.

140. R.H. Charles, *The Revelation of St. John*, ICC, Vol.II, p.148. He can only imagine 'that the heavenly Jerusalem here referred to was to descend before the disappearance of the first earth and the first heaven and the final judgment described in 20.11-15'. Thus Charles combines 20.1-3; 21.9-22,2,14,15,17; 20.4-15. Only afterwards does there follow the destruction of the old world and the new creation, 21.5a,4d,5b, 1-4abc; 22.3-5. But since in chs.20-22 the language of John is recognizable, Charles concludes, 'that John died either as a martyr or by a natural death, when he had completed 1-22.3 of his work and that the materials

for its composition, which were for the most part ready in a series of independent documents, were put together by a faithful but unintelligent disciple in the order which he thought right' (Vol.II, p.147). A similar disciple-figure is used by P. Gaechter, 'The Original Sequence of Apocalypse 20-22', *Theological Studies* 10, 4, 1949, pp.485-521.

141. E. Lohmeyer, *Die Offenbarung des Johannes*, Handbuch zum NT, ²1953, p.167. Lohmeyer wants to see in 21.5a the end of the apocalyptic part and in 21.9ff. an independent vision which 'ihre Prägung von den Bedrückungen der Gemeinde in der Gegenwart des Sehers empfängt' (p.169).

142. In Rev. 21.9 only the seven bowls are more precisely characterized according to 15.1.

143. Neither in Rev. 17 nor 21 are different 'sources' worked together. Lohmeyer's division of 21.1-5a (as the seventh image in the vision series of 'perfection') and 21.5b-22.7 (made the 'promising part' beside the 'apocalyptic part', 4.1-21,5a, and the 'hortatory part', 1.9-3.22) is the unfortunate result of his artificial arrangement of the whole book in a number of sevenfold units.

144. The voice from the throne and the voice of God are clearly distinguished. The first voice speaks of God in the third person; the voice of God speaks of himself in the first person.

145. Cf. J. Comblin, *La liturgie de la Nouvelle Jerusalem*, Publications universitaires, Löwen 1953, and C. Brütsch (see n.74), Vol.III, pp.10ff.

146. Cf. I B 6-7.

147. The sea as the home of the demonic powers is to be distinguished from the lake of fire.

148. The heavenly city is probably originally heaven itself, the city of the gods whose precious stones are the stars and whose street and river is the Milky Way, and whose twelve gates are connected with the Zodiac; cf. R. Knopf, 'Die Himmelsstadt', *Neutestamentliche Studien. Georg Heinrici zum 70. Geburtstag*, T.C. Hinrich'sche Buchhandlung 1914, pp.213-9; F. Dijkema, 'Het hemelsch Jeruzalem', *Niew Theologisch Tijdschrift* 15, 1926, pp.25-43; A. Causse, 'Le mythe de la nouvelle Jerusalem du Deutero-Esaie à la 3e. Sibylle', *Extrait de la Revue d'Histoire et de Philosophie religieuses*, Nov.-Dec. 1938, pp.1-38; H. Strathmann, *TDNT*, VI, pp.531-3; B. Meissner, *Babylonien und Assyrien*, Vol.II, C. Winter 1925, pp.107ff., 409ff.

149. Cf. J. Behm, *TDNT*, III, pp.449f.

150. For the details cf. my book, *Time and History*, pp.96-103.

151. We observe the same ambivalence in the interpretation of the Jerusalem traditions with Paul and in Hebrews.

152. Cf. n.150.

153. Rabbinic traditions probably express the same thought when they speak of Jerusalem's reaching up to the throne of God; cf. Strack-Billerbeck, IV, pp.921f.; Eth. Enoch 58.5; 51.4f.; 62.15.

154. On Jewish apocalypticism, cf. D. Rössler, *Gesetz und Geschichte*, Neukirchener Verlag 1960, pp.95-100.

155. Cf. also Jer. 31.34; Zech. 8. The OT passages fully suffice to

104   *The Future of the World*

explain the idea of 'marriage' used in 19.7; 21.2. It is unnecessary to trouble with the myth of a *hieros gamos*. Cf. also II Cor. 11.2; Eph. 5.25ff.; Mark 2.19; Matt. 22.2ff.; 25. 1ff.; John 3.29.

156. W. Bousset, *Die Offenbarung Johannes*, KEK, 1906, p.444, speaks of a mosaic of OT passages and motifs.

157. Cf. Jer. 31.33; Ezek. 37.27; 48.25; Zech. 2.10f; 8.8. Tobit 13.10 also speaks of God's 'tent' in the New Jerusalem. The tent among men as 'bildkräftige Bezeichnung für die dauernde Gegenwart Gottes' does not contain any suggestion of an eschatological dwelling of God's people in tents, as W. Michaelis has rightly emphasized (*TWNT* VII,pp.7,382). The text tradition of v.3c is uncertain. The variant αὐτοὶ λαοὶ αὐτοῦ is perhaps a mistake of a copyist caused by the similarity to αὐτοί.

158. The combination of death and sufferings, cries and pain proves that the notion does not point here to a personified power of death (so also rightly W. Michaelis, *Die Versöhnung des Alls*, p.168, n.71). For Jewish analogies cf. H.W. Kuhn, *Enderwartung und gegenwärtiges Heil*, Studien zur Umwelt des Neuen Testaments 4, Vandenhoeck und Ruprecht 1966, pp.104ff.

159. τὰ πρῶτα is identical with ὁ πρῶτος οὐρανὸς καὶ ἡ πρώτη γῆ (21.1).

160. Cf. I A, 2.

161. The variant γέγονα (and γεγόνασιν) is certainly secondary. On the reasons for the origin of the reading γέγονα (which 'fälschlich im Sinne von εἰμι zum folgenden gezogen wurde' in the text forms in which εἰμι is missing) cf. J. Schmid, *Studien zur Geschichte des griechischen Apocalypse-Textes*, Vol.II, K. Zink-Verlag 1955, p.94.

162. A similar formula with the same meaning is related also to Christ: 'the first and the last' (1.17; 2.8). 'The beginning of God's creation' in 3.14 is especially interesting because the creation appears here connected with the absolutely valid word (here of the witness Christ, the 'Amen').

163. It is significant how the apocalyptist refers to the creation.

164. The classification of 22.13 among the words of Jesus (22.12ff.) allows for the transfer of the divine formula to Jesus.

165. With the elimination of the hope for a future re-creation of the world, the whole biblical belief in the creation in its all-embracing significance collapses.

166. Cf. Zech. 14.8; Isa. 55.1. The eschatological promise of 21.6 is characteristically related to the present in 22.17, for in the church the eschaton has already begun in a hidden fashion (cf. 3.1).

167. In Heb. 1.5 related to Christ. In Rev. 21.7 'father' is replaced by 'God', since God is called the Father of Jesus exclusively (1.6; 2.28; 3.5,21; 14.1).

168. The list consists of seven parts and one summarizing formula ('and to all liars'). Lying as a perversion of everything that is true and valid (opposite of v.5) is the primeval sin (cf. the emphasis on lying in 2.2; 3.9; 14.5). Lohmeyer (*Comm.*, p.169) compares with that John 8.44 ('the devil is a liar from the beginning'). The individual concepts in the list probably stem from traditional *Lasterkatalogen* (cf. commentaries on

Rom. 1.28ff.). It is striking that 'cowardice' is placed first — suggesting the struggle of the church in the world.

169. Cf. n.155.

170. It seems doubtful whether this combination of the two pictorial words belongs to the original text or whether it is a later harmonizing. The original text probably spoke (in view of 21.2) parabolically only of the 'bride'. The combination of 'bride' and 'wife' was easily possible because 'the designation of the bride as γυνή is in keeping with current Palestinian usage' (J. Jeremias, *TDNT*, IV, p.1099). The 'parallel' Esd. 7.26 *apparebit sponsa apparescens civitas* is certainly a miswriting; cf. H. Gunkel in E. Kautzsch, *Die Apokryphen und Pseudepigraphen des A.T.*, J.C.B. Mohr 1900, Vol.III, p.370 and J. Jeremias, op. cit., IV, p.1102.

171. φωστήρ has here the unusual meaning 'light', 'radiance' (cf. 4 Esd. 8.79) and so this is parallel to δόξα (cf. R.H. Charles, *Comm.* Vol.II, pp.161f.).

172. Cf. Ps. 104.2 and Exod. 24.17, and on this T. Boman, *Hebrew Thought Compared with Greek*, SCM Press and Westminster Press 1960, pp.88f. Jasper is either green or gray or purple or reddish or white or blue (like the blue of the sky), according to Pliny, *Natural History*, XXXVII, 115f.

173. In John 2.21 the concept of the temple is related to the earthly Jesus. It is significant for Rev. 21 that the title of the sacrificial lamb appears in this cultic context!

174. Cf. O. Michel, *TDNT*, IV, p.889.

175. Cf. n.148 also; R. Reitzenstein, *Das iranische Erlösungs-mysterium*, Bonn 1921, pp.188ff.; K.L. Schmidt, *Die Polis in Kirche und Welt* (cf. n.97), p.31 and his contribution, 'Jerusalem als Urbild und Abbild', in *Eranos-Jahrbuch*, Vol. 18 (1950), p.227.

176. I Kings 6.20; II Chron. 3.8f.; according to Exod. 36.34 even the boards of the tabernacle were covered with gold. This naturally does not exclude the possibility that the Holy of Holies of the temple itself was influenced by Oriental ideas of heaven. The cubic shape of Jerusalem is known also by the Mishnah Tractate Baba Bathra 75b.

177. B. Meissner, *Babylonien und Assyrien*, Vol.II, C. Winter 1925, pp.107,110.

178. Rev. 4-5; 6.9; 7.9-17; 8.1-6; 15.1-8. On the Jewish tradition of a pre-existent Jerusalem, cf. II A, 2. Here John differs from Gal. 4 and Heb. 12. This is rightly emphasized by G. Dalman (*Die Worte Jesu*, Vol.I, J.C. Hinrich'sche Buchhandlung 1898, p.106): 'Auch im Neuen Testament sind die Aussagen von dem "oberen" oder "himmlischen Jerusalem" (Gal. 4.26; Heb. 12.22) mit den Aussagen von dem vom Himmel kommenden Jerusalem Offb. 3.12; 21.2,10 keinesweges zu kombinieren.' Not only does the heavenly Jerusalem never appear before ch.21, but it belongs exclusively to the new heaven and the new earth.

179. I Kings 8.10-13; Ezek. 45.3. P. Carrington, *The Meaning of the Revelation*, Macmillan 1931, p.346, notes (although he gives a different interpretation of the whole image): 'The cubic shape is probably based on the Holy of Holies in the temple.'

180. Cf. E. Lohmeyer, *Comm.*, p.173, who calls the numbers 12,000 and 144 'relics of an old tradition' which is no longer understood. The relation to the history of salvation (Israel) is much more essential for John's Revelation than is the 'cosmic relation' (so R. Halver, *Der Mythos im letzten Buch der Bibel*, H. Reich Verlag 1964, p.111).

181. E. Lohse, p.46.

182. The name of the sealed ones, 'the servants of God', which is the common name for church members in 2.20; 6.11 (cf. K.H. Rengstorf, *TDNT* II, pp.323-5) also speaks for this interpretation.

183. So, for instance, L. Goppelt, *Christentum und Judentum im ersten und zweiten Jahrhundert*, C. Bertelsmann 1954, p.120: 'Die Offenbarung, das Buch von der Endgeschichte der Gemeinde, schweigt auffallenderweise über die heilsgeschichtliche Zukunft des jüdischen Volkes' (cf. also p.262).

184. Perhaps Paul thinks here of the church.

185. Cf. n.150.

186. Whereas the words in 21.5-8 directed to the church are formed according to the number 7.

187. G. Klein, *Die zwölf Apostel*, Vandenhoeck und Ruprecht 1961, pp.75-80, rightly points to this 'primäre Interesse (des Apokalyptikers) an der in aller Variabilität der Bilder konstanten Zwölfzahl'. This, of course, does not exclude the possibility that the twelve apostles (21.14) are for the author already an element of the tradition (so rightly: W. Schmithals, *Das kirchliche Apostelamt*, Vandenhoeck und Ruprecht 1961, p.233).

188. Cf. A. Feuillet, *L'Apocalypse*, Stud. Neotest. Subsidia 2, Desclée de Brouwer 1963, pp.48-52.

189. Cf. L. Goppelt, *Christentum und Judentum*, p.261. Paul recognizes in the hostile attitude of the Jews toward the gospel, and therewith toward himself and the Christian church, the sign of their hardening. Israel has become the persecutor of the gospel (cf. J. Munck, 'Christus und Israel, Eine Auslegung von Röm. 9-11', *Acta Jutlandica*, XXVIII, 3, 1956, pp.42-6). For John, the true situation of Judaism without Christ is disclosed in the enmity of the Jews of Smyrna and Philadelphia (2.9; 3.9).

190. The preservation of a remnant of Israel is a significant motif also in Rev. 12 (cf. n.150) and for Paul (Rom. 11.5); cf. C. Müller, *Gottes Gerechtigkeit und Gottes Volk*, Vandenhoeck und Ruprecht 1964, pp.45-7.

191. Cf. A. Feuillet, 'Essai d'interpretation du chap. 11 de l'Apocalypse', *NTS* 5, 1958, pp.183-200; and n.150. Israel's constant encounter with the gospel is also essential for Paul's considerations in Rom. 9-11 (Rom. 10.14-21). In Rom. 10.21 the same situation as in Rev. 11.3ff. is described by Paul with the quotation from Isa. 65.2:

> I spread out my hands all the day
>   to a rebellious people,
> who walk in a way that is not good,
>   following their own devices;

On this cf. especially J. Munck, 'Christus und Israel', p.61. Paul, however, speaks more of the redeeming word which is refused, while Rev. 11 speaks above all of the judging power of the redeeming word whose witnesses are rejected.

192. The three-and-a-half times of Dan. 7.25 and 12.7, which also appear with the number of months and days in the Revelation, limit the time of the woman's preservation (12.6,14), the activity of the two witnesses (11.3) and the Antichrist (13.5). The end of this time is the parousia of Christ, which terminates the sufferings of the church and the power of Satan and Antichrist (19.11ff.). Even this (the third element) is also to be found in Rom. 9-11. The hardening of Israel lasts ἄχρι οὗ τὸ πλήρωμα τῶν ἐθνῶν εἰσέλθη (Rom. 11.25). Perhaps the judgment εἰς τέλος in I Thess. 2.16 is also limited: 'till the end' (cf. Heb. 6.11). Nevertheless, the agreement of the traditional elements of Rom. 11.25f. with Rev. 11 may not be as direct as C. Müller, *Gottes Gerechtigkeit und Gottes Volk*, pp.42f., asserts. Paul does not know the idea of an abandonment of Israel into the hands of the nations even in a spiritualized form, for the nations do not 'vollstrecken das Gericht an Israel dadurch, dass sie es vorläufig vom Heil ausschliessen', but God alone. Moreover, Rev. 11.13 would scarcely suggest an association with the restitution of Israel, since the city, according to 11.9, houses heathen people, and the formula 'they became fearful and paid homage to the God of heaven' is here rather an expression of naked fear (so, rightly, D.W. Hadorn, *Die Offenbarung des Johannes*, Theologischer Handkommentar zum NT, XVIII, Deichertsche Verlagsbuchhandlung 1928, p.123). The designation of God used here occurs in post-exilic Judaism (G. Dalman, *Die Worte Jesu*, 1898, p.143), but remains rather a sign 'bewusster Anlehnung an fremde Religion' (W. Bousset-H. Gressmann, *Die Religion des Judentums im späthellenistischen Zeitalter*, J.C.B. Mohr [3]1926, pp.312f.). Therefore it is not to be expected in the mouth of a *converted* Israel, since this predicate of God appears in Rev. 11.11 in connection with the blaspheming enemies of God (never in the rest of the New Testament)!

193. Cf. 1.6; 5.10; 7.1-8; I Peter 1.1; James 1.1.

194. Paul, too, sees the restitution of Israel in the context of a new creation and resurrection (Rom. 11.15).

195. E. Lohmeyer, *Comm.*, p.36.

196. Cf. n.150.

197. 7.16f.; 21.6; 13.8; 21.27. This is probably the reason why the number 7 (in the structure of the vision) plays a role at least in the background (cf. II B, c).

198. In Isa. 60 only the open doors are mentioned, and in the New Testament concepts of the heavenly or future Jerusalem the wall does not play any role at all (Gal. 4.26; Heb. 11.10; 12.22; 13.14); in the Jewish tradition the wall serves as a defence for the city.

199. Cf. Isa. 60! The wall has nothing to 'protect', as Bousset thinks (*Comm.*, p.447).

200. Bousset, *Comm.*, p.451, declares that Rev. 21.24 does not fit with the preceding statements because here a 'without' is presupposed. He thinks of an archaic trait which originally belonged to the earthly Jerus-

108 *The Future of the World*

alem concept (cf. p.454). The apocalyptist has quite consciously worked
the traditional traits into an overall picture. Of course, the hortatory
statements in 21.8,27; 22.15 refer to the church on earth, but they
presuppose the idea of a 'within and without' which begins with the
parousia of Christ (C. Brütsch [see n.74], Vol.III, p.44, does not pay
attention to this).

201. The name of the leader of the underworld discloses the nature of
his kingdom: his goal is the destruction of God's world.

202. Cf. I B, 5.

203. Rev. 19.20; 20.14f.

204. Cf. I B, 5.

205. Rev. 20.10. In 14.10 the eschatological judgment is also referred
to, as the wording suggests; cf. 20.10. So also W. Michaelis, *Versöhnung
des Alls*, p.108.

206. Cf. my *Time and History*, pp.30-33.

207. Paul also uses the plural αἰῶνες, when he speaks of a limited but
incalculable time (I Cor. 10.11); cf. on the whole problem especially O.
Cullmann, *Christ and Time*, SCM Press and Westminster Press 1962,
pp.61-8; W. Michaelis, *Versöhnung des Alls*, pp.41-3.

208. So rightly against W. Hadorn, *Die Offenbarung des Johannes*,
p.203; W. Michaelis, op. cit., pp.110f.

209. The message to the church in Smyrna is dominated by the
life-death motif (cf. 2.8; 10.11). Cf. 20.6,14 (in v.14 the identification of
the lake of fire and the second death is probably a secondary expansion of
the text); 21.8. On the pre-history of the notion of the second death, cf.
Strack-Billerbeck, III, p.830.

210. Cf. 6.7.; 21.13.

211. There is no mention of a battle with the powers of the world of the
dead.

212. Cf. 6.9-11; 7.9-17; 15.2-4.

213. W. Michaelis, *Versöhnung des Alls*, p.115.

214. Rightly emphasized by Michaelis, op. cit., pp.100-102.

215. Lohmeyer prevents himself from understanding the text when he
concludes from 21.24-7: 'der Bestand der ersten Erde und mit ihr ihre
Könige und Völker (sei hier) vorausgesetzt' (*Comm.*, p.169). He therefore
has to take refuge in his strange distinction of two different kinds of
visions.

216. Cf. II A, 2.

217. ἐνδώμησις apparently here means the material of the wall (cf.
Josephus, *Antt.* 15, 9.6 and inscriptions).

218. 21.14. The seer apparently thinks of huge blocks of precious
stones just as he also pictures the gates as enormous pearls. Cf. Eph. 2.20;
Heb. 11.10.

219. Cf., for instance, the commentary of Andrew about the stones:
ὧν οἱ ὀκτὼ ἐν τῷ λογίῳ τοῦ ἀρχιερέως πάλαι ἀνεφέροντο, οἱ δὲ τέσσαρες
παρηλλαγμένοι εἰσιν, ἵνα φανῇ καὶ τὸ σύμφωνον τῆς νέας πρὸς τὴν
παλαιὰν καὶ τὸ ὑπερέχον τῶν ἐν αὐτῇ διαλαμψάντων. He then distributes
the precious stones among the various apostles. Text according to J.

Schmid, *Studien zur Geschichte des griechischen Apokalypsetextes*, Pt. 1, *Der Apokalypsekommentar des Andreas von Kaisareia*, K. Zink-Verlag 1955, p.243.

220. Cf. F. Boll, *Aus der Offenbarung Johannes. Hellenistische Studien zum antiken Weltbild der Apokalypse*, Leipzig-Berlin 1914, pp.39f.; C. Clemen, *Religionsgeschichtliche Erklärung des N.T.*, Töpelmann 1909, p.79; Charles, *Comm.*, Vol. II, pp.165-9; Caird, *Comm.*, p.277. They think of connections with zodiacal speculations. To the contrary and rightly Lohmeyer, *Comm.*, p.174. A thorough study of the precious stones mentioned in Revelation is provided by U. Jart, *The Precious Stones in the Revelation of John 21.18-21*, Studia Theologica 24, 1970, pp.150-81. The theological problems of the stones, however, are not really solved.

221. H. Rusche has rightly pointed to this trait in his article about the heavenly Jerusalem in *Lexikon für Theologie und Kirche*, Vol.V,[2] 1960, p.368.

222. Cf. B. Reicke, 'Die Verfassung der Urgemeinde im Lichte judischer Dokumente', *ThZ* 10, 1954, pp.95-112 (esp. 104f.). The circle of the Twelve has again been removed from the life of Jesus in recent discussions (cf. already Wellhausen, *Einleitung in die drei ersten Evangelien*, G. Reimer 1911, pp.138ff.), and its origin transferred to the time after Easter (P. Vielhauer, 'Gottesreich und Menschensohn', *Festschrift für G. Dehn*, 1957, pp.62-4; W. Schmithals, *Das kirchliche Apostelamt*), or even to the theology of Luke (G. Klein, *Die zwölf Apostel*). Cf. against this K.H. Rengstorf, *TDNT* II, pp.325-8; G. Bornkamm, *Jesus of Nazareth*, Hodder and Stoughton 1960, p.150. We cannot enter into the discussion here, since for the interpretation of Rev. 21, the question of the origin of the circle of the twelve apostles is not essential.

223. The motif of judgment is also connected with the twelve apostles in Matt. 19.28.

224. Isa. 62.6:   Upon your walls, O Jerusalem,
                    I have set watchmen.

225. Similarly Baba Bathra 75b.

226. Rev. 21.25. The explanatory addition 'for there shall be no night' belongs to the Johannine interpretation of Isa. 60.

227. That the names of the disobedient should not be erased is an expression of God's faithfulness. Cf. the interesting inscription of the eighth century which warns against erasing a name (H. Donner and W. Röllig, *Kanaanäische und aramäische Inschriften*, Harrassowitz, Vol.I, 1962, p.5 and Vol.II, 1964, pp.35-43; 'Wenn aber ein König . . ., wenn ein Mensch, der ein angesehener Mann ist, den Namen des 'ZTWD auslöscht von diesem Tore und einen (andern) Namen (darauf) setzt . . ., so möge der Baal des Himmels und El, der die Erde geschaffen hat . . ., jenen König auslöschen.'

228. ῥίζα is to be understood in this way here and in 22.16 – already in the MT, Isa. 11.10 (cf. C. Maurer, *TDNT* VI, pp.986f., 989).

229. So, for instance, Bousset (*Comm.*, 256): 'Die ganze Schilderung des Messias zeigt noch einige urwüchsige, ungewohnte Züge eines national

orientierten Judenchristentums.' But it is as little a question of this here as it is in the gospels, which understand Jesus in the light of the Old Testament revelation history.

230. Cf. G. Schrenk, *Die Weissagung über Israel im Neuen Testament*, Gotthelf-Verlag 1951, pp.16f. In Acts 3.20f. we also find the hope for the coming of a time of salvation for Israel, probably on the basis of the Elijah prophecy in Mal. 4.5f. (cf. B. Reicke, *Glaube und Leben der Urgemeinde*, 1957, pp.69-71). The tradition here demands the repentance of Israel as the necessary preparation for the coming of the Messiah (cf. H. Conzelmann, *Die Apostelgeschichte*, Handbuch zum NT, 1963, pp.34f.) and thus clearly reckons with the restitution of God's people before the parousia. The same form of the hope for Israel appears also to be present in Matt. 23.29.

231. Cf. esp. K.L. Schmidt, *Die Judenfrage im Lichte der Kapitel 9-11 des Römerbriefes*, EVZ 1943; J. Munck, 'Christus und Israel'; K. Barth, *Church Dogmatics* II, 2, T. & T. Clark 1957, pp.213ff.

232. A. Schlatter, *Gottes Gerechtigkeit. Ein Kommentar zum Römerbreif*, Calwer-Verlag ² 1952,p.327.

233. For the interpretation cf. O. Michel, *Der Brief an die Römer*, KEK, 1955, pp.250f.; U. Luz, *Das Geschichtsverständnis des Paulus*, Beiträge zur Evangelischen Theologie 4, C. Kaiser-Verlag 1968, pp.286-300.

234. G. Delling, *TWNT* VIII, p.56.

235. I Cor. 15.24-7. καταργεῖν cannot here mean 'destroy', for it stands in parallelism with ὑποτάσσειν (which is also used of Christ in relation to God, v.28) and appears in the interpretation of the image of Ps. 110.1, which does not point to destruction but to submission (cf. G. Delling).

236. The interpretation of this verse is disputed; cf. O. Michel, *Der Brief an die Römer*, pp.241f.

237. Cf. the discussion by K.L. Schmidt, *Die Judenfrage*, pp.40ff.

238. A. Schlatter, op. cit., p.327.

239. With this, Paul reaches out beyond the scope of the Old Testament formula 'all Israel' (used by G. Schrenk, *Die Weissagung*, p.35).

240. J. Jeremias, *Jesus' Promise to the Nations*, Studies in Biblical Theology 24, SCM Press. ² 1967, p.60.

241. It is striking that John does not follow here the terminology of Isa. 60 which very often speaks of kings, but substitutes the expression 'the kings of the earth', which is taken from Ps. 89.28 (cf. Ps. 2.2) and is treated throughout the book as a fixed entity. Caird, *Comm.*, p.279, gives a similar interpretation: John 'did not believe that God would be content to save a handful of martyrs and allow the rest of mankind . . . to perish in the abyss.' Brütsch (see n.74), Vol.III, pp.55-64, follows our explanation as a whole, although he is afraid to pursue the line John draws from the parousia to the redemption of all. The question is not whether we want to construct 'a logical system', but whether we want to acknowledge that John is not only a collector of apocalyptic traditions or a sick visionary, but a thinker of hope who places his expectations upon the revelation of

God in Jesus Christ.

242. J. Jeremias, *Jesus' Promise to the Nations*, p.70.

243. Cf. I A, 3.

244. E. Lohmeyer, *Comm.*, p.175.

245. This interpretation is not to be found in pre-New Testament documents. The closest parallel is probably 1QH8, 20ff. John 7.38 speaks of the 'streams of living water' which shall flow out from the believer. Cf. P.H. Reymond, *L'eau, sa vie, et sa signification dans l'Ancien Testament*, E.J. Brill 1958, pp.234-8.

246. Cf. Zech. 14.8; Joel 3.18; J. Jeremias, *Golgotha*, 1926, pp.54-8,60-64,82-5.

247. K.H. Rengstorf, *TDNT* VI, pp.604f.

248. Gen. 2.9. ξύλον ζωῆς is to be understood collectively, as in Ezek. 47.12 (cf. Gen. 1.11); Rev. 2.7.

249. Bousset, *Comm.*, p.450 understands ἡ πλατεῖα τῆς πόλεως in a generic way: 'alles, was die Stadt an Strassen hat'.

250. Michaelis (*Versöhnung*, p.111) seeks to find in 21.4 and 20.14 'zwei verschiedene Stadien im Schicksal des Todes', and he concludes: 'Im Zeitpunkt von 21.4 hat das bequältwerden, hat der Aufenthalt im Feuersee für den Tod ein Ende gefunden. Der Tod ist nun überhaupt nicht mehr da.' But under this interpretation the destiny of the other powers would not yet be decided. What is more important, however, is that his whole interpretation cannot be maintained, for the termination of death (21.4 does not speak, as we have seen, of 'death' as a person) is connected neither with the condemnation of Thanatos and Hades according to 20.14 nor with their dissolution in the lake of fire (there is no mention of it), because for the redeemed death is already abolished before his fall into the lake of fire (in the first resurrection, 20.6), and after the parousia of Christ there are only 'dead' and 'resurrected' ones, but no longer any 'dying'.

251. Cf. H.P. Müller, 'Die himmlische Ratsversammlung', *ZNW* 54, 1963, pp.254-67.

252. The universality of the statement of 5.13 is for many commentators an embarrassment which they try to overcome by removing all angels and men from the cosmos and letting only fish and birds rejoice! But the parallelism with the threefold formula in 5.3 excludes this interpretation. But, above all, the function of the mighty concluding hymn has to be considered, in which all choirs of the visions in chs. 4 and 5 join together with all creatures: because now the victor who had been sought with tears has been found, the victor who can accomplish what no one in all the realms of creation was able to do. Therefore, the jubilation embraces *all* creatures without exception.

253. In 4.8, *trisagion*, the three predicates of God and the threefold formula of time; in 4.11, threefold acclamation and threefold description of the Creator.

254. In 5.12, sevenfold acclamation; in 5.9, fourfold development of the victory of the Lamb by means of four verbs and a fourfold formula describing mankind; in 5.13, the cosmos is divided into four realms, and

God and the Lamb are praised in a fourfold formula.

255. Here again the kinship between the Johannine and the Pauline hope appears, for Paul's discussion of the destination of the history of salvation ends with a prospect of the mercy which God will show to all: Rom. 11.32-36 (cf. Rom. 5.18; I Cor. 15.22, where the two πάντες stand parallel to each other without distinction of meaning). Because at the end 'all' will be in Christ and brought to life through him (I Cor. 15.22), because all powers and enemies of Christ will be subordinated to him, therefore God will be at the end πάντα ἐν πᾶσιν (I Cor. 15.28). Because John and Paul think in the light of the same reality, namely, Christ crucified and risen, they agree in their motivation and in the unfolding of their eschatology, in spite of their different spiritual backgrounds.

256. Cf. II B, a.

257. Cf. 7.3; 9.4; 14.1; and 3.12.

258. Cf. J. Comblin, *La liturgie de la Nouvelle Jerusalem*, p.18.

259. Cf. F. Horst, *ZAW* 47, 1929, pp.50-54; G. von Rad, *Old Testament Theology*, Vol.I, Oliver & Boyd and Harper & Row 1967, pp.357ff.

260. L. Köhler, *Theologie des Alten Testament*, J.C.B. Mohr 1947, p.208.

261. Bousset also, who elsewhere makes a different division of the material, sees in 22.16 the beginning of a 'Schlusswort zum Ganzen' (*Comm.* 458).

262. E. Lohse (see n.138), p.105. Charles, *Comm.* II, p.221, has not understood the meaning of the word: 'Here the door of hope is closed absolutely and finally against every class of sinner.' He therefore wishes to understand the verse as a later interpolation.

Index of Authors

Index of Biblical References